Postcards of the Army Service Corps 1902–1918

Coming of Age

Postcards of the Army Service Corps 1902–1918

Coming of Age

Michael Young

Pen & Sword
MILITARY

First published in Great Britain in 2016 by
Pen & Sword Military
an imprint of
Pen & Sword Books Ltd
47 Church Street
Barnsley
South Yorkshire
S70 2AS

ISBN 978 1 47387 813 6

A CIP catalogue record for this book is available from the British Library

Typeset in Ehrhardt by
Mac Style Ltd, Bridlington, East Yorkshire
Printed and bound in Malta by Gutenberg Press

Pen & Sword Books Ltd incorporates the imprints of Pen & Sword Archaeology,
Atlas, Aviation, Battleground, Discovery, Family History, History, Maritime,
Military, Naval, Politics, Railways, Select, Transport, True Crime, and Fiction,
Frontline Books, Leo Cooper, Praetorian Press, Seaforth Publishing and
Wharncliffe.

For a complete list of Pen & Sword titles please contact
PEN & SWORD BOOKS LIMITED
47 Church Street, Barnsley, South Yorkshire, S70 2AS, England
E-mail: enquiries@pen-and-sword.co.uk
Website: www.pen-and-sword.co.uk

Contents

Acknowledgements

First and foremost, I must thank Colonel Michael McHenry, late US Army Transportation Corps, co-author of *"Badges of the Empire's Waggoners"* and himself a considerable expert on the history of our Corps, not only for suggesting I should produce this book, countering all my arguments against but also then giving help and advice most generously thereafter. There is no doubt that without that support I would have led a quieter life these past two years or so and this book would never have seen the light of day. Such good friends are hard to come by.

As ever, thanks are due to the Institution of the Royal Army Service Corps and Royal Corps of Transport, successor Corps to the Army Service Corps, for their generous support, not forgetting their faith in my ability to 'produce the goods'.

I am also greatful for advice from David Kellock, who kept me 'on the straight and narrow' when it came to obscure details of Volunteers early in the twentieth century; to Rod Dux in Australia for his skilled and practical comments on my work; and to Bertrand Revert in France for his leading me towards a more imaginative title than would otherwise have appeared. "No man is an Island" and the book is better for the influence of each and every man mentioned above, almost a support team in themselves.

Glossary

AMR: Army Motor Reserve
AOD: Army Ordnance Department
ASC: Army Service Corps
CBE: Commander of the Most Excellent Order of the British Empire
CO: Commanding Officer
Co or Coy: Company
DSO: Officer of the Distinguished Service Order
EFC: Expeditionary Force Canteens
FC: Forage Corps
FWD: Four Wheel Drive
GS: General Service
HT: Horse Transport
HQ: Headquarters
hp: Horse Power
lbs: Pounds (in weight)
LGOC: London General Omnibus Company
MAC: Motor Ambulance Convoy
MT: Mechanical Transport or Motor Transport
MTV: Motor Transport Volunteers
MVC: Motor Volunteer Corps
NCO: Non-Commissioned Officer
OC: Officer Commanding
OHMS: On His (or Her) Majesty's Service
p.c. : Postcard
QMG: Quarter Master General
RA: Royal Artillery
RASC: Royal Army Service Corps
RE: Royal Engineers
RSM: Regimental Sergeant Major
T: Territorial
SE: South East
TF: Territorial Force
UK: United Kingdom
V: Volunteer
WO: Warrant Officer
YMCA: Young Men's Christian Association

Introduction

It is some thirty-five years ago, when I was serving with the Army in Scotland, that a handful of Army Service Corps postcards came into my possession; with my life-long interest in history, it struck me immediately that they were more than just junk pieces of card. Indeed, I recognized that they were historic artefacts, arguably to be rated alongside the more serious photographs to be found in national and regimental archives.

There is, however, a key difference between museum photographs and postcards: whereas archive photographs were largely taken by professional photographers for official use, postcards were produced for unit and individual private use, to communicate with others, families and friends. These postcards, often with messages on the reverse, have a more human appeal and illustrate scenes that a professional photographer would not dream of recording; however, they tended to be worn or damaged through use over the years and were frequently thrown away, if only because they were not deemed to be worth keeping. Or so people thought. Today, we know otherwise, as recognised by the thousands of people who collect postcards, for all sorts of reasons, and the number of postcard clubs that exist not only in this country, but around the world.

In the United Kingdom, collecting postcards is big business, with its own professional association, network of full-time and part-time dealers and a profusion of fairs around the country every weekend. Some people buy cards of subjects such as actors, animals, artwork, churches, deckchairs, flowers, ships, railway stations, soldiers, street scenes, villages and windmills – the list is endless. Nowadays, old postcard albums are highly sought after, not thrown away as they were. With hindsight, it is clear that the period between the turn of the century and 1918 were golden days for military postcards, especially during the First World War, when huge numbers of men and women served in the Royal Navy, the Army and later the Royal Flying Corps – they were uprooted from home and wanted to stay in touch. Strangely enough, this flood of postcards was not repeated during the Second World War – among other reasons, the airgraph was introduced, something not feasible earlier.

My own interest centred on all aspects of the ASC, which turned out to be almost prophetic as, some ten years later, I became the Curator of the museum in Aldershot, which represented the predecessors and successors of the ASC. Among the Corps archives was a host of photographs, predominantly excellent official photographs – the difference between these and my cards was glaringly obvious.

At the same time as becoming Curator, I became the Editor of the Corps magazine, *The Waggoner*, one of the oldest regimental magazines in the Army. I immediately insisted that any photographs submitted for the magazine were retained for the Corps archives, thus adding to our collection. Something I learnt early on was that, while those who received the magazine read only a very limited proportion of the contents, every single person looked at every single photograph; as a result, the number of photographs published in each issue increased from around forty to about two hundred in a period of a year or so, a deveopment that attracted wide acclaim.

A few years after I retired, I produced *Army Service Corps 1902–1918*, published by Pen & Sword, in which a number of my postcards were used, along with a selection of photographs from the Corps archives of course. Those illustrations were key factors in that book's appeal, something mentioned by several reviewers. This new book, *Postcards of the Army Service Corps 1902–1918*, can be considered in some ways complementary to its predecessor, in that it goes one stage further by concentrating purely on illustrations, all of which I collected as postcards over those thirty-five years. Informative captions and footnotes bring many to life and add to our appreciation of the 500 plus photographs published here that show the final days of the ASC before its elevation as a Royal Corps and illustrate, to a certain extent, its development and world-wide involvement.

A few illustrations appear in both the earlier book and this one, but I have no hesitation in doing this since every photograph in this book has been repaired or digitally restored so that each one is now closer to the standard of photograph as seen by the original sender about a hundred years ago. All the photographs in my first book show damage, scratches, tears, creases and a variety of marks, incurred by wear and tear over the years, as do all photographs in virtually every other historical book. The difference after restoration is quite remarkable, the result of moving into the twenty-first century through the acquisition of new technology.

It will be seen that the illustrations are largely arranged chronologically, with a semblance of grouping, in chapters that seem to provide natural divisions. It will also be seen that some cards defied restoration efforts, but at least the effort has been made. Taken as a whole, the images reflect the world as experienced by ASC men at the time, which will give the reader a better understanding of the Corps and what life was like for its men compared with just reading words. Many are informal photographs of no importance at all, photographs that would never otherwise be seen in official collections, yet they are well worth their place; others are as good and important as professional photographs in archives. There is a place for all types of scenes to bring us to an understanding of what it was like to be a serving soldier during the period 1902–1918, whether Territorial or Regular. We can learn so much by studying photographs.

Unfortunately, cards were not produced showing every activity of the ASC, so the odd gaps will be evident to the knowledgeable reader; much more noticeable, however, is the regrettable paucity of cards from overseas theatres of war, with the exception of the Western Front. Places such as East Africa, the Balkans, the Dardanelles, Russia, even Palestine, had few or no photographic establishments, either to take photographs or to produce postcards, so the limited number that appear were largely printed either later at home or in India. The photographs reproduced in the last chapter reflect this situation, not a reduced interest in the activities in overseas theatres of war.

A limited number of illustrations show the reverse of cards sent from training units in the London area, purely to show what individuals thought at the time; it is also interesting to look at their handwriting and savour the expressions used. Sadly, the majority of cards have nothing of interest to say, although one has to smile ruefully with little snippets, such as when a husband sends a card to his wife from annual camp a good distance away saying he will arrive home 'today'. Things are certainly not what they used to be. Cards sent from overseas during the war were subject to censorship, of course, which led to only the most mundane of messages getting past the censor's red pen.

When it came to photographs of soldiers before 1914, Territorials are far better represented than their Regular counterparts since, in the main, they gathered together only once a year for annual camp, when local photographers seized the opportunity for a bit of trade and profit, the results of which are collected and appreciated today. Regular soldiers, in contrast, invariably appeared during a tasking of some sort, often with vehicles which were still an interesting distraction for the population at large, but they were in smaller groups. Photographs overseas after 1914 did not differentiate between the two, except for those Territorial Divisions that existed in peacetime and recruited only in their local areas, although that changed progressively as reinforcements were increasingly posted in. Interestingly, vehicles appeared more often on postcards than horse transport, which was perceived as being a routine almost boring sight every day, while vehicles were something of a novelty on the roads of this country. It has to be said, though, that the photographs of horse transport are generally of a better quality and their men are better turned out than those of MT units; postcards that show vehicles, however, are significantly more expensive to buy today than those of horse transport.

To the best of my knowledge, only the ASC served in every theatre of war and also had such a wide range of duties and equipment to justify a book like this. That is not to say that other regiments or Corps were uninteresting or unimportant, quite the opposite, but they did not produce the number and variety of cards to compare with the ASC. There is no question, of course, that units and men of the ASC were more widely seen and in greater numbers than most, which partially accounts for the large number of ASC cards that can be bought at weekend fairs or by means of the computer today.

It is difficult to imagine that the soldiers of 1902–1918 would not be fascinated by the images in this book, if only they were with us today; neverthelesss, I hope you gain new insights into a large but not well-known Corps, and at the same time can identify with the individuals concerned and enjoy their photographs. Unbeknown to them, they have inadvertently become the subject of arguably the most photographed regiment or Corps in the period before and during the First World War.

Evolution of the Army Service Corps 1794–1918

Logistic functions as carried out by the Army Service Corps (ASC), essentially transport and supply, had been performed over hundreds of years, but it was only in 1794 that a formal, uniformed Corps was raised by the British Army to support the expeditionary force in the Low Countries, commanded by the Duke of York, to fight with the Austrians and Prussians against the French.

The first royal warrant of 7 March 1794 authorised the creation of a **Corps of Waggoners**, also known as the **Royal Waggoners**, with just 5 companies and some 500 men, to serve under the civilian Commissariat in support of the Army, led by Captain Commandant James Poole. Recruiting virtually the dregs of society as they did was not an auspicious start for a newly-formed Corps to go abroad to help fight a war; the situation was not helped either by then taking part in an ignominiously unsuccessful campaign in the Netherlands, but it was a beginning. At the end of the campaign, British Forces returned to England and the Royal Waggoners were disbanded. No war, no logistic support needed.

In 1799, another British expedition went to North Holland, this time to try to break the French hold on the strategically important Scheldt estuary. A **Royal Waggon Corps** was formed under Waggon Master General Digby Hamilton to support this move, but Treasury parsimony obstructed the provision of wagons, so it is not surprising it was reported that they were inadequate for the needs of the Army. Fortunately, the French soon proposed an armistice and the Army quickly returned to England. Strangely, there appears to have been some difficulty in deciding on a name for the Corps and variously **Royal Waggon Corps**, **Corps of Waggoners** and **Corps of Royal Waggoners** appear in documentation of the time. In 1802, however, when the Corps was located in Canterbury, the title **Royal Waggon Train (RWT)** appears to have been selected, appearing in 1803 in Army Lists as a mounted corps below the 29th Dragoons, the junior cavalry regiment, and senior to all Guards regiments, Infantry of the Line, Royal Artillery and Royal Engineers. It soon had a strength of 2,000 men, including 120 armed Privates, although these numbers were soon reduced. The RWT, fortunately, did much better than its predecessors, although it was responsible only for the provision of transport, supplies being the responsibility of the Commissariat, a civilian service that was responsible for providing supplies, both food and forage, under the control of the Treasury, employing officer-status civilians using local contractors.

In 1807, the Emperor Napoleon invaded Spain and Portugal, which then appealed to Britain for help. After initial reverses suffered by the British Expeditionary Force under General Sir David Baird, Sir Arthur Wellesley, later the Duke of Wellington, took another force to Portugal, including the RWT and Commissariat. They saw extensive and increasingly successful service under the Duke of Wellington in the Peninsula, France and Belgium, culminating in the Battle of Waterloo in 1815. The defeat of Napoleon made the threat of war in Europe virtually non-existent, and it was clear that economies were necessary, so the RWT was reduced to two troops in 1818 and eventually disbanded in 1833. So ended the early steps to provide a permanent transport service for the British Army, not the first or indeed the last time economies were necessary in order to save money in a time of peace.

The outbreak of the Crimean War in 1854 found the British Army neglected and disorganized, significantly without uniformed logistic support, which led to great suffering and privation when British troops landed in a country that could not provide the essentials of life for an initial force of about 26,000, in spite of the best efforts of the Commissariat. The weather was appalling, there was no transport organization and the supply situation was dire. The government fell when news of this scandalous situation became known in England, but the new government began to set things right: the Commissariat was transferred from Treasury control to the War Office and an organization entitled the **Land Transport Corps (LTC)** was established in April 1855 under the command of Colonel William McMurdo, who was clearly a master organizer. With seven Divisions in the Crimea, seven all-military regiments of the LTC provided support, each regiment consisting of two battalions, a Transport Battalion and a Commissariat Battalion, the success of which helped change the situation completely. The strength of a regiment, at best, was some 45 officers, 1,175 men and 1,562 horses. It was the start of a number of changes throughout most of the remaining years of the century.

At the end of the Crimean War in March 1856, the LTC was reorganized in August and renamed the **Military Train (MT)**, still commanded by Colonel McMurdo; the new organization, having returned to England, was based in Bristol. What was important, however, was that there was again a general recognition, perhaps due to the Train's outstanding performance in India at the time of the Indian Mutiny, where two Victoria Crosses were won, that a permanent transport organization really was needed in the Army; but there was still a separation of responsibility for transport and supplies. Initially there were only three Train battalions, totalling 27 officers, 480 men and 546 horses, many of the men coming from cavalry regiments, but this establishment was shortly increased to six battalions and in 1865 to 24 troops, each troop consisting of 71 officers and men, and 41 horses, now based in Aldershot.

Following the Crimean War, no less than seventeen Royal Commissions and nineteen War Office Committees examined the supply and transport needs of the Army. The result of these deliberations was the formation in 1869 of the **Control Department**, which consisted of officers who had previously served in the **Commissariat & Transport Department** and a small **Army Service Corps** (ASC) consisting of twelve horse transport companies. (The title Army Service Corps lasted longer than any other Corps name, until 1965, with the grant of the 'Royal' prefix in 1918 as a result of its performance in the First World War.)

The remaining years of Queen Victoria's reign saw a number of minor involvements abroad, in China, New Zealand and Abyssinia, but the main events were the Zulu War in 1879, where a third Victoria Cross was awarded, the first Anglo-Boer War of 1880–1881 and later the second Anglo-Boer War of 1899–1902, in all of which campaigns virtually the whole British Army took part, including most of the ASC.

1888 saw an important organizational change, indeed a turning point in the Corps' history, when the officers, who had meanwhile served in a series of Commissariat Departments, and the men of the ASC were amalgamated, with the War Department Fleet, to become the (second) ASC, a fully combatant Corps. Officers and other ranks served together in a permanent, unified and military organization for the first time since Royal Waggon Train days; this was undoubtedly the result of influence by General Buller, the Quarter Master General of the day, who had witnessed the efficient performance of the ASC in the Red River Expedition in Canada in 1870. At the same time, the Commissary General and his entire staff were abolished and promotion prospects for the officers were greatly improved. The first head of the 'new' Corps was Colonel HSE Reeves. The ASC rapidly developed a true regimental identity and *esprit de corps*, with a red brick officers' mess and accommodation blocks replacing the wooden hutted camp in Aldershot, as well as new family quarters built adjacent to the barrack blocks.

The end of the 19th century saw the development of mechanization throughout Europe and America, and the Royal Engineers (RE) led the way in the British Army, operating a limited number of vehicles, mainly steam traction engines. In 1901, a War Office Mechanical Transport Committee, chaired by Brigadier FT Clayton (late ASC), was formed 'to consider and compare various types of self-propelled vehicles which appear suitable for the Army'. At about the same time, mechanical transport (MT) was made the responsibility of the Army Service Corps, which took over a small number of vehicles from the RE; trials were immediately held in Aldershot in 1901 to evaluate possible vehicles. Two of the prize winners, a Thornycroft steam lorry and a Foden lorry, were sent to South Africa in 1902 for field trials, with other trials being held in subsequent years in England. Several staff cars were acquired too for trials with senior officers in 1902.

That year of 1902 was a key moment in the evolution of the ASC, since a small MT Section was officially authorized as well as the first two MT units, 77 and 78 (MT) Companies, which were subsequently formed in Aldershot in 1903 and 1904, manpower being provided by reductions in four Horse Transport Companies. The next MT Company was formed in 1908 and two new MT Companies were formed every year until 1914, with the exception of 1911. In due course, a variety of vehicles were trialled, including steam traction engines and motor cycles.

It was also in 1902 that promotion to Colonel was authorized for ASC officers, which opened up the possibility of senior appointments that had not previously been possible, particularly in the War Office. That the work of the ASC and its senior officers was increasingly appreciated by the Army led to a further significant step: in 1904, the Army Council accepted that ASC officers 'would be eligible equally with officers of other arms, thus giving opportunities of promotion to general officer's rank'. Within five years the Corps could claim four Major Generals, which greatly improved its position in the Army as a whole.

In 1902, at the end of the second Anglo-Boer War, the ASC consisted of sixty-five Horse Transport (HT) Companies, of which thirty-nine were in South Africa and twenty-six in the UK, along with two **Remount Companies** and five **Supply Companies**. Five HT Companies were located in Aldershot, seven in Woolwich, three in Dublin and one each in Chatham, Cork, Curragh, Devonport, Dover, Dublin, Manchester, Portsmouth and Southampton. The units at home were all at lower (or cadre) strength, somewhat less than half their full establishment. There was, of course, an overall framework of headquarter staffs, from the Quarter Master General's Department in the War Office cascaded down through the various Command, District and Garrison Headquarters at home and in overseas garrisons.

Volunteer soldiers had long played an important role in the Army, but it was only after the Anglo-Boer War of 1899–1902 that a few Volunteer HT companies appeared in the ASC, initially supporting a limited number of County Volunteer Brigades. In addition to this support, other Volunteer organizations were formed, which were not linked with or allocated to specific formations: in 1903, the **Motor Volunteer Corps (MVC)** came into being 'to provide a pool of professional and owner drivers who would be willing to offer their time and their automobiles to the service of the Army in various districts of the country'. In practice they conveyed individual staff officers at various Command Headquarters around the country and provided more comprehensive support on annual manoeuvres. The MVC disbanded in 1906, but were immediately replaced by an all-officer **Army Motor Reserve (AMR)**, with a similar role, which in turn disbanded in 1913, by which time serving soldiers were providing the same service.

In 1908, there was a comprehensive reorganization of the Volunteers in the Army, renamed the **Territorial Force (TF)** in April. The ASC was established with Transport & Supply Columns to support Divisions in the twelve military Districts in the United Kingdom: the Highlands, Lowlands, East Lancashire, West Lancashire, Wales, Northumbria, West Riding, North Midlands, South Midlands, Wessex, East Anglia, Home Counties and (with two Divisions) London. Each Column, totaling some 500 men, had 4 Companies, the No 1 (HQ) Company and a Transport Company attached to each of the three Infantry Brigades in the Division. Each Division also had a smaller (c.112 men) Transport & Supply Column ASC to support its Mounted Brigade. The more understandable (and shorter) title 'Train' replaced the lengthier 'Transport & Supply Column' throughout the ASC in 1915.

All ASC TF transport units supporting Territorial Divisions operated only horse-drawn transport before and during the First World War, although an MT Company was attached during the war, essentially to carry the amount of heavy ammunition required by the Royal Artillery. In contrast, the Regular ASC operated not only Horse Transport, but also a variety of MT vehicles, starting with cars and 3-ton lorries, added to by workshop lorries, steam traction engines, ambulances and fire engines before the war.

Inevitably, the war introduced other functions, which in turn required different vehicles, equipment and animals: Holt caterpillars to pull heavy guns, disinfectors to kill off bugs in soldiers' uniforms, petrol tankers to provide bulk fuel for the large number of MT vehicles in use, vans for general administration, and even London omnibuses to replace shank's pony for the movement of troops; more unusual were threshers, ploughs and potato diggers for the Agricultural Park in Salonika, motor boats in the Middle East, armed motor boats in Salonika and armed canal boats in North Russia. Types of animals not used by the British Army before were also brought into service: camels in Egypt, reindeer in North Russia and mules and donkeys in a variety of places. Flexibility and adaptability were key words in ASC circles.

The number of companies and other units formed and disbanded during the war is difficult to present, but an impression of the demands placed on the ASC during this can be deduced from the fact that, after the declaration of war, 133 new transport companies were formed in 1914, 409 in 1915, 264 in 1916, 164 in 1917 and 134 in 1918. Total Corps strengths varied greatly also, but after the 6,431 officers and Other Ranks serving in August 1914, 325,881 was the highest figure reached in 1918; the Corps operated 56,659 lorries, 23,133 cars and vans, 7,045 ambulances, 5,400 tractors, 1,285 steam wagons and 34,865 motor cycles during the war. A host of other statistics could be provided to illustrate the development of the Corps in response to the needs of the Army, but the above figures suffice to make the point. Major General SS Long was head of Corps as the first Director of Supplies & Transport in 1914; Major General AR Crofton Atkins followed him in March 1916.

When HM King George V visited the British Expeditionary Force in 1914, he enthused about the ASC with Lord Kitchener, the Secretary of State for War, who decided to keep such views under wraps but, in November 1918, the king noted with great satisfaction the splendid work done by the Corps and commanded that the title 'Royal' should be bestowed on the Corps. Looking back at the Corps' hesitant start from 1794 onwards, and the various changes that took place throughout the reign of Queen Victoria, it can truly be said that royal recognition of their significant achievements during the First World War signified the moment when the Army Service Corps really came of age.

Chapter 1: Early Years: 1902–1908

View of Stanhope Lines in Aldershot, showing Mandora Barracks, with the 1879-built Cambridge Military Hospital on the skyline. Buller Barracks, effectively the home of the ASC since the late 1850s, is out of sight further to the right.

18 and 63 Companies at Thorn Hill Camp in Buller Barracks, Aldershot in 1907. At that time, 18 Company was stationed in London and 63 Company in Belfast. Of interest are the three large bays in the left background, built to house the first ASC workshops and the early steam tractors.

The 'Tramlines' (see footnote 1) housed the HQ offices of the Service Companies of the ASC Training Establishment. 'W' Square is located on the other side of these offices. This card is one of a set of six cards of Buller Barracks published by Gale & Polden in 1904 (see footnote 2).

A royal visit to the Aldershot Supply Depot in 1904. Being greeted is Princess Helena, Duchess of Albany (1861–1922); behind her is Prince Alexander of Teck (1874–1957) and Princess Alice of Albany, later Countess of Athlone, whose husband became the Governor General of Canada from 1940 to 1946.

The HQ ASC building in Woolwich, next to the guardroom. Woolwich was second only to Aldershot as an important Corps station, mainly responsible for Horse Transport (HT) and associated trade training.

A Sunday church parade in front of the main Royal Artillery building in Woolwich. The ASC Band can be seen on the right.

Steam Thornycrofts lined up, of the type that won the £500 first prize in the 1901 War Office MT trials. One of these vehicles had been sent to South Africa in 1902 for trials during the Boer War of 1899–1902.

Four early cars lined up in Kensington Barracks in London, c1903. Left to right: a 12 hp Wolseley (used by members of the Army Council), a 12 hp Lanchester (used by the Chief Royal Engineer), a 6 hp Wolseley (used by the Commander 1st Army Corps) and a 12 hp Siddeley (used by the Commander 4th Army Corps). The number plates starting with A indicate the cars were registered in London.

Lieutenant General Sir John French in a 1905 London-registered (LC-837) 12 hp Wolseley, at annual manoeuvres in 1907 in Aylesbury, Buckinghamshire. His ASC driver wears a white dust-proof overcoat.

1904 Army manoeuvres saw the disembarkation of a force by the Royal Navy at Clacton-on-Sea, supported by 26 and 52 Horse Transport Companies (HT) based in Aldershot. A team of soldiers is unloading a heavy load, with a GS wagon on the right, probably waiting to cross-load stores. ASC motor transport was also used for the first time, including cars of the Motor Volunteer Corps (see footnote 3).

A 1904 card of a group of the Sussex & Kent Volunteer Brigade ASC, probably the guard. The officer with the sash on the right may well be an inspecting officer or the Regimental Colonel. The men are wearing Kilmarnock caps, used from the 1830s until the early 1900s, when the Brodrick Cap replaced them (see footnote 4). Prior to the 1908 ASC reorganisation , such ASC companies existed in Volunteer Brigades.

An Army Service Corps Terrritorial unit on manoeuvres in 1907. Note the white shoulder titles used in the Corps until 1908. Each Company had several of its own GS wagons, but the non-standard wagons (and their horses) illustrated were hired from local Territorial Associations for annual camp.

The King's Birthday parade on Laffan's Plain in Farnborough (see footnote 5), normally a training area. A Horse Transport Company drives past with GS wagons, mounted officers leading the way. Other units taking part can be seen in the background, including another ASC Horse Transport Company.

The Royal Review of September 1905 at the Palace of Holyrood in Edinburgh, when twelve cars of the Motor Volunteer Corps, formed in 1903, were inspected by HM King Edward VII. Three of the cars can be seen centre left.

Working staff of the Supply Depot in Buller Barracks, Aldershot in 1904. 122 men appear in the photograph, with a mixture of headdress and uniforms.

Cattle about to be slaughtered in the Aldershot Supply Depot in 1904. The sender of the card wrote, 'These animals have long since been duly sampled by Tommy Atkins' (see footnote 6). The Warrant Officer wearing the striped apron on the right can be seen in the previous photograph.

a. Supply Co. a S C. Aldershot, 1906.

'A' Supply Company, Aldershot 1906, consisting of 53 men, including two officers, a Warrant Officer and Trumpeter, strangely enough holding a trumpet and a bugle. The trumpet was the official instrument of the ASC as a mounted Corps. All those below Warrant Officer rank are wearing the unpopular Brodrick Cap.

A Field Bakery in Aylesbury during annual manoeuvres in September 1907, with Aldershot ovens (see footnote 7) and a new mobile oven in the background.

A covered GS wagon with two postilion riders in Woolwich in 1904.

Trumpeters in Woolwich in 1904, with their NCO-in-charge, none of them looking particularly happy – life was hard for them. Until 1914, trumpeters were in Boys' service, before eventually progressing to Man's service and either joining the Corps Band or taking up a trade. Boys' service in the Army was a great boost for any young man about 15 years of age, leading eventually to improved chances of promotion.

The Wheelwrights' Shop in Woolwich in 1904, where the trade was taught to ASC personnel. All ASC Wheelwrights were trained in Woolwich in the construction and repair of wooden wheels etc.

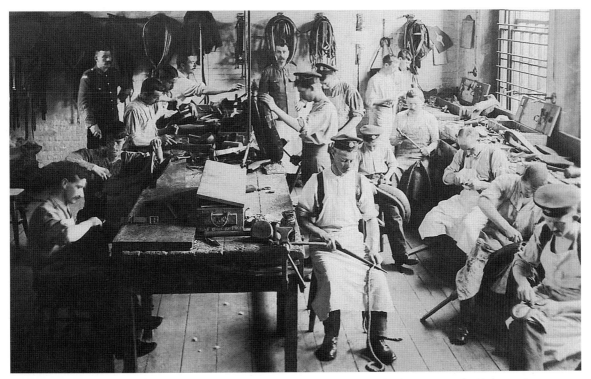

The Saddlers' Shop in Woolwich in 1904, with two uniformed instructors. Horse collars can be seen on the wall as well as being worked on by several men. All ASC Saddlers were trained in Woolwich in the construction and repair of all equine leather equipment before and during the 1914–1918 war.

72 Company on manoeuvres in Coate Camp near Swindon. On the left is a Wallis & Stevens 'Small' traction engine (ASC 22) next to a motor cycle registration LN2748 and a privately owned bicycle. In the background are three office trucks, part of the Repair Train Workshop Section.

A group of Warrant Officers, Staff Sergeant Majors and a Sergeant in No 1 Dress, with a mixture of Royal (Victorian) and Tudor Crown helmet plates. All medals are from the Boer War 1899–1902.

The wife of Colonel FWB Landon, Officer Commanding (OC) ASC Aldershot, presents prizes at the annual Corps Sports Day on 'God's Acre' (see footnote 8), in front of the HQ ASC HQ Officers' Mess (see footnote 9) in Buller Barracks, Aldershot, c1908.

Pushball being played on 'God's Acre' in Buller Barracks, Aldershot in 1907 (see footnote 10), part of the entertainment during the Corps Weekend festivities. The game was invented in Massachusetts, USA in 1891 and was introduced in England in 1902, at the same time as pushball on horseback was also introduced, played only in military tournaments such as at Olympia. The game died out after 1918.

The dinner table laid for a formal Dinner Night in the Officers' Mess, Woolwich, c1904. Corps Officers and Sergeants Messes held various silver pieces that had been presented for a variety of reasons and sports trophies, which they displayed on appropriate occasions. The mess waiters were long-serving civilian staff, some of whom were almost certainly ex-Corps members.

The ASC parading in the Cavalry Barracks, Aldershot before marching to Sunday church. Piles of hay outside the horse stables can be seen on the left, with accommodation for the soldiers above them.

An early parade of Service Company men on 'W' Square (see footnote 11), probably for the Colonel-in-Chief, His Royal Highness The Duke of Connaught, son of Queen Victoria. GS wagon bays and stables are at the bottom of the parade ground. 'W' Square terrified ASC and RASC soldiers over the years, although its reputation was always worse than its bite, depending on your rank.

A more informal parade on 'W' Square c1908, with Lee Enfield rifles, probably a Monday morning first parade. The majority on parade are Mechanical Transport men (wearing the 1903 leather belts), along with Horse Transport men (wearing bandoliers), with a cook in whites and a plain clothed soldier with a rifle.

A smart HT man.

A proud Sergeant with his son.

Mixed uniform, c1912.

A Boy Trumpeter, about 15 years old.

Rehearsal for the ASC Wagon Mounting & Dismounting competition at the 1906 Royal Irish Military Tournament in Dublin, early days in this type of competition (see footnote 12).

The ASC Band leads the Sunday Church Parade back from St George's on Queen's Avenue to Buller Barracks, Aldershot, c1910. Church parades on Sundays or appropriate days were compulsory.

Relaxing in barracks, c1907, with personal photographs seen above their bed spaces. Three men are wearing the Brodrick Cap.

A 19 Company group in Middleburg, South Africa in 1908, where it had been stationed after taking part in the 1899–1902 Boer War, before it moved to Dublin in 1912.

Chapter 2: The Pre-War Years: 1908–1914

Officers, a Warrant Officer and NCOs display their newly-won shooting cup in Woolwich c1908. Most have Anglo-Boer War 1899–1902 medals or ribbons.

A Farriers' Course at the Army Veterinary School in Aldershot in October 1908. There are two ASC permanent staff and five ASC students.

Regimental representatives, including three ASC officers (centre left), follow the cortège on Queen's Avenue, Aldershot on the occasion of the funeral of Captain Charles Beresford RE in 1910. The Corps Church of St George (see footnote 13) can be seen centre top. Note the photographer on his stepladder on the left.

A 1910 view of Thornhill Camp, Buller Barracks, Aldershot. Note the open-sided cookhouse shelter is probably for the unit moving in for its annual camp. The old Supply Depot buildings can be seen in the centre.

A unit day outing in Portsmouth, probably 12 (HT) Company, for which occasion a carriage from Southsea has been hired. Cases for a stringed instrument and an accordion can be seen in front of the line of men. (And isn't it strange how often someone appears at a window when a photograph is being taken?)

Thornhill Camp to the right of the old Supply Depot is packed with tents, looking towards Camp Farm. The Basingstoke Canal runs across the centre of the photograph by the scrubland.

This Swiss Moto-Rève (registration LN4308) was not accepted by the Army MT Committee (see footnote 14).

An MT group in 1912 in Aldershot, probably a course for car drivers. The subaltern with the dog is Lieutenant Bertram Rowcroft, who was selected in 1942 as the first head of Corps for the newly formed Royal Electrical & Mechanical Engineers (REME).

Annual camp of the East Lancashire Supply & Transport Column ASC (TF) in Carnarvon in 1914.

A Territorial Force unit at camp, c 1910. The left-hand GS wagon is standard Army issue, but the three other visible wagons and horses will have been hired for camp through their Territorial Force Association.

The (Highland) Division Transport & Supply Column (TF) at camp in Kingussie, c1912. It is interesting to see a crowd of about thirty at the far end, presumably local people watching the activity.

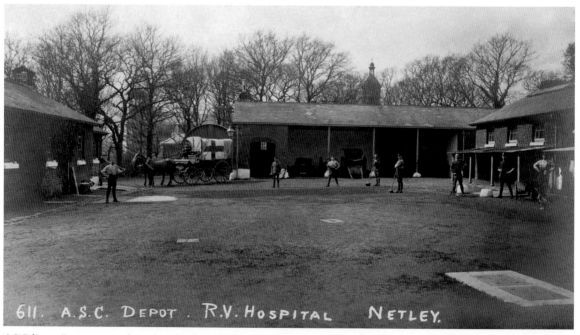

ASC lines (it was not a depot) at the Royal Victoria Military Hospital Netley, near Southampton, established in 1856. Beneath the hospital's foundation stone, laid by Queen Victoria, lies the first Victoria Cross.

'Preparing the Downy Couch' at camp in the Portsmouth area in 1911, palliasses being filled with straw in a barn. The ASC were responsible for providing all visiting units with straw at annual camp for this purpose.

No 4 Bakery at camp in Bisley, Surrey in 1910, with a fine display of recently baked bread.

Blacksmiths demonstrate their skills working with metal at annual camp.

A Territorial Force ASC Driver, 'N Beckworth', with a hay-filled GS wagon in the yard, c1914. His 3-bar shoulder title reads, 'T/ASC/Cheshire', indicating he was in the Cheshire Company (strength 2 officers and 97 men) of the Welsh Division Transport & Supply Column (TF).

48 ASC men carry wreaths in the funeral procession for Colonel Sam Cody on 11 August 1911 on Lynchford Road, Farnborough (see footnote 15).

The same wreath carriers pass St George's Church on Queen's Avenue, Aldershot.

The wagon on which Colonel Cody's coffin was carried was provided by the ASC. Note the small boy (bottom left) is about to doff his cap.

The 'Giant Caterpillar' travelling at 4 mph, c1907, the Army's first tracked vehicle. At 20 tons, the Hornsby from Grantham was too heavy and slow for the Army and was dismantled in 1914. It was called the 'Giant Caterpillar' or 'Walking Engine'.

Side view of the 'Giant Caterpillar', which took part in the 1907 MT trials in Aldershot. It had been converted from wheels to tracks at the request of the Army MT Committee.

The 'Baby Caterpillar' seen here in the Larkhill area of Salisbury Plain, c1912. It had been bought in 1910 for £870.00 from Hornsby & Sons and was on the strength of 74 Company in Aldershot (see footnote 16).

A group of Gunners and ASC men during trials at Larkhill. The three ASC men are the ones without jackets and the rest are gun crews taking part in the trials. One of the guns and some shells can also be seen.

An ASC 75 hp Fowler 'Lion' traction engine, 'The Great Bear', probably in Melksham, where the ASC had its traction engines overhauled.

Another 75 hp Fowler, 'Joan of Arc', without its superstructure.

A Fowler 'Ursula' from 74 Company in Aldershot after a slight accident with a bridge over the River Arrow in Herefordshire (see footnote 17).

A Foster 'Small' steamer and trailer, said to be outside a Strong's Romsey Ales pub in King's Somborne, Hampshire.

A 'Light' Foster steam engine No 51 in 73 Company in The Curragh, Ireland. It had been bought in 1908 for £492.00 and was registered in Southampton (AA-2246).

A Foden steam lorry carries hay for No 3 Veterinary Field Section of the Army Veterinary Corps. The men on top must have had an interesting ride.

This photo of 64 Company ASC (MT), commanded by Captain FGG Moores, was probably taken in January 1912 in Bulford when 63 Company ASC (MT) was renumbered as 64 Company (MT) (see footnote 18).

Two gun detachments of the Royal Artillery in Malta, with two ASC Aveling & Porter 'Small' steam engines (Nos 46 and 47) in support costing £450-00 each. The steam engines towed these guns to what appears to be a training area north west of Valetta, c1910.

This was the first Territorial Force group to undergo training in Buller Barracks, Aldershot in November 1908, when the Territorial Force was reorganized on a regimental basis (see footnote 19).

An Aveling & Porter steam engine (ASC 46) with a Douglas motor cycle and an office truck (ASC 6) seemingly used for stores, in the training area north west of Valetta.

26 Company (HT) was stationed in Aldershot in the period 1903 to 1914. This photograph shows the four trophies won in 1910.

The Band of the ASC at the head of a funeral procession in Station Road, Aldershot, c1910. Aldershot railway station, built in 1870, can be seen in the background, essentially unchanged today.

ASC-driven horsed ambulances supporting the RAMC on manoeuvres, c1908.

A GS wagon from 10 Company, the only ASC unit stationed in Colchester before the Great War, is decorated very unusually with flowers and greenery for the funeral of a unit soldier.

FUNERAL OF S.S. MAJOR ROWFELL. A.S.C.   SILK 9.

The funeral of 1st Class Staff Sergeant Major Rowsell in Eastney, Hampshire on 10 December 1910. He had been Chief Clerk in the Land & Water Transport Office in Gunwharf, Portsmouth.

A Field Bakery at annual camp on Salisbury Plain, c1912, with bread ovens at work. The sign behind the loaves reads 'Casey's Court', a reference to entertainment in twentieth century Britain (see footnote 20).

GS wagons lined up for inspection in front of a large ASC crowd, probably in Aldershot. This was probably a display by Company teams that wished to compete at Olympia.

A wagon mounting & dismounting competition, a preliminary competition in preparation for Olympia, held on the Recreation Ground in Buller Barracks, Aldershot.

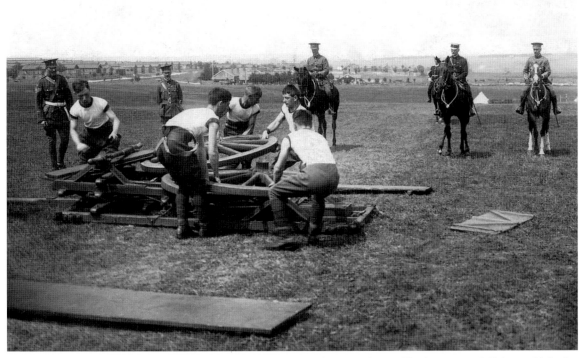

Unusually, wagon mounting & dismounting is taking place in the Bulford area on Salisbury Plain by members of either 15 or 22 Companies (HT) stationed in Bulford, neither of which ever won at Olympia.

A wagon mounting & dismounting team stand behind a dismounted wagon on the ASC transport park in the Royal Victoria Hospital Netley in Hampshire on 30 June 1911.

Two ASC teams at Olympia for an early wagon mounting & dismounting competition. Judging by the empty stands, this was a rehearsal during daytime in preparation for the evening performance (see footnote 21).

Four teams stand easy during an evening performance at Olympia.

GS wagons unloading stores into office trucks, which were used as stores wagons at Olympia. The ASC possessed nine office trucks, two of which were with 70 Company in Malta. They were not used after 1914.

A Territorial Column at annual camp in Bridlington, in the East Riding of Yorkshire, c1912, with the 1841-built Priory Church of St Mary in the left background. The men are in the process of weighing hay.

A Territorial unit, probably an element of the Northumbrian Division Supply & Transport Column ASC (TF), parades in Preston Park, near Stockton-on-Tees to celebrate the coronation of King George V.

A Mark XI GS wagon, with a pair of immaculate horses. Note that the driver is not wearing spurs, both in this and the other GS wagon photographs in this book, since they could injure the horses in an accident.

An empty GS wagon of the North Midland Division ASC (TF). It appears that the No 1 Driver has given a lift to two infantrymen and, in order to give them room, rode the lead horse himself (without spurs).

The 1st London Division ASC (TF), probably on day one of annual camp. The left-hand GS wagon must have been permanently held by the Column, as indicated by the lettering painted on the side.

A two-in-hand and one postilion team with mules and a dog at annual camp, c1912. The GS wagon of this time cost about £60.00 to produce.

A Merryweather fire engine (AA 5054) stands outside the fire brigade building on Queen's Avenue, Aldershot, with another older fire engine behind it as well as a horse-drawn GS wagon used as a fire engine.

The ASC provided fire brigades in all Army garrisons in the UK and overseas. This photograph shows the Army Fire Brigade on Queen's Avenue, Aldershot, c1910. Two horse-drawn fire engines can be seen, with the ASC providing the drivers and escort and local volunteers acting as firemen.

MT and HT fire engines on show on Queen's Avenue in Aldershot.

Two horse-drawn fire engines in front of the 'Aldershot Camp' bays, with the ASC drivers and civilian voluntary fireman teams.

The Guards' Dash to Hastings in 1909. As can be seen, crowds gathered by the roadside to cheer them on (see footnote 22).

The Guards on the open road south, well wrapped up against the winter cold. 'Hastings, here we come!' The LC registration number of the lead car indicates it was registered in London.

An airline wagon (see footnote 23), a GS wagon modified for the Royal Engineers, used on this occasion by the ASC, in front of Corfe Castle in Dorset. The castle was built in the time of William the Conqueror in the 11th century and was partially demolished on the orders of Parliament in 1646.

Young Territorials at camp weighing wood for the Aldershot ovens. Each oven required up to 400 lbs of wood a day, distributed by these young soldiers.

Seven empty GS wagons in line, and one right at the back, almost certainly on a training run. A Staff Sergeant Major walks at the front, while there are five mounted escorts spread evenly alongside the column.

Four loaded GS wagons on a narrow country road in the Folkestone area, possibly on their way to camp in late summer, c1912.

A line of Fowler traction engines from 74 and 78 Companies ASC on a task in Bordon. Both companies were based in Aldershot, Hampshire, c1910.

A relaxed group of men from 74 Company in the MT bays in Buller Barracks, Aldershot. The white ASC shoulder titles worn by the seated man on the right indicate a date of about 1908.

A photograph of 75 Company on its formation in June 1910 in The Curragh, Ireland. It shows the company at Lower Establishment, shortly after the death of King Edward VII in May 1910 (note the black armbands worn by the officers and (probably) the Staff Sergeant Major 1st Class). Two steam engines can be seen, a Fowler 'Lion' (ASC 15) and a Fowler 'Light', as well as a Triumph motor cycle.

A Foster 'Small' from 78 Company, Aldershot. ASC No 43 cost £477.00 when it was bought in 1906. The load appears to be agricultural. The photographer was H Leach, a well-known Aldershot photographer.

Members of an Infantry unit are filling their palliasses with straw provided by the ASC. The young girl on the right with a basket full of food is perhaps the daughter of one of the men.

Territorials take a break while setting up camp. (A pity the photographer's writing is indecipherable.)

A line of interesting vehicles in Aylesbury, Buckinghamshire. On the left are a 12 hp Wolseley car, a 5-ton Milnes-Daimler and a Straker-Squire ambulance; beyond them is a variety of steam engines, including Fowlers, a Wellington tractor, a Garrett tractor, a Burrell crane and a mobile office trailer.

Four Fowler 'Lion' Traction engines on detail at West Down Camp on Salisbury Plain in 1909. 'ASC 10' from 77 Company in Aldershot can be seen second from the right; it had cost £1426.00. West Down Camp is a wooden-hutted camp on the bare and wind-swept hills of Salisbury Plain, still in use today.

Tents of the West Riding Transport & Supply Column at camp, c1912. A free Sunday on the middle weekend and a warm day provide the opportunity to do the laundry and hang it all on the line to dry.

A Territorial unit cleaning tack at camp. The Corporal on the left wears four Territorial Force Proficiency Stars which denote a possible twenty years of proficient service (see footnote 24).

A range party of Farriers at camp.

A GS wagon ('240 Coy ASC 11' is stencilled on its side) delivers the baggage of the King's Own Yorkshire Light Infantry in Brocton Camp, Staffordshire. 240 Company was formed in February 1915 for local duties in the Cannock Chase and Lichfield area, disbanding in March 1920.

Members of a Horse Transport unit being served a meal at speedily erected tables at camp in 1914. The lumps of meat do not look very appetizing, but hopefully they are at least cooked.

Better organized this time, admittedly for smaller numbers.

A relaxed boxing match between fellow Territorials at annual camp. The referee, with the cloth cap and stop watch in the centre, is taking things seriously, the kneeling corners with their compulsory towels also.

These men are probably the mobile guard at camp, with Lee Enfield rifles secured onto their bicycles, which enabled them to cover a large area quickly. Such Army bicycles used to be called 'bog wheels'.

A group at camp: Private Coyne (Butcher), Corporal Trotle (Baker), Driver Gould , 2nd Lieutenant Tapp (looking somewhat grim), Lance Corporal Thompson (Butcher), Corporal Kelly (Clerk) and Driver Teffer.

Another Regular group at camp, also using bales of hay. Note the soldiers copy officer habits by having turn-ups on their trousers; and officers never seem to smile for the camera.

An ASC hired GS wagon delivers supplies to a Royal Artillery unit at camp. Identifiable are a carcass, meat on sacking on the ground, a loaf of bread, cheese and assorted jars. Two of the four ASC drivers (wearing bandoliers) are carrying rifles.

More meat on display at camp, with a fine selection of containers.

Men of the South Western Brigade of the Wessex Division ASC waiting patiently while in Bulford Camp, Salisbury Plain, 1912, perhaps thinking of the weekend to come.

Guard mounting by a Horse Transport unit at Windmill Hill Camp, near Ludgershall on Salisbury Plain, 1910. Rolled blankets are for night-time warmth.

The Reserve Supply Depot ASC of the North Midland Division, including beef, eggs, bread, cheese, bacon, tins of Peaman's peas @ 2d each and tins of Commodore herrings. Contents of the Butcher's Kit can also be seen.

An Infantry tented camp beside the seaside, supplied by a lorry and GS wagon of the ASC.

Bacon, loaves of bread and an 80lb bag of ASC salt are on display here at this Regular camp.

Men of the 2nd South Midland Mounted Brigade display their supplies at Park Hall Camp in Oswestry, c1912, including Huntley & Palmer biscuits, sides of beef, bacon, Colman's mustard, Fray Bentos corned beef and bread, as well as 50lb of jam and 60lb of marmalade in boxes. Park Hall Camp was used as a prisoner-of-war camp during World War One, the last German prisoner leaving in November 1919.

Weighing supplies at camp. A tin of Fray Bentos beef is visible centre right. The dog looks well fed.

Whether at home or in camp, the laundry needs to be done, certainly here near Tidworth on Salisbury Plain, c1912. The right-hand man, with two irons ready in front of him, is perhaps drying his own 'long johns'.

48006 : ALDERSHOT, STANHOPE LINE Y.M.C.A.

The YMCA Hut (see footnote 25) in Stanhope Lines, Aldershot must have been known to generations of ASC men, with limitless tea and cakes, writing materials and Russian billiards.

Members of the Sergeants Mess of the 1st London Division ASC at annual camp, c1912. The two boys are probably the sons of Mess members.

Territorials relax on a sunny day. Uniforms and bedding are given an airing. The kit bag (bottom right) shows the initials 'WBMB ASC' (Welsh Border Mounted Brigade), part of the Welsh Division ASC (TF).

A miserable (dreich for the Scots) day at camp, with waterproofs essential for survival.

A Territorial unit deploys to camp perhaps, or out on a weekend exercise, taking a short break. Note the fire trailer and mules. (This is the first of four sequential photographs of this particular unit.)

The passing Lieutenant sees it all: the two men on the right draw water for their horses from the stream below and one horse is about to be given its water in a nosebag (in the centre).

All attention seems to be focused on the man in the centre with what looks like a box, though it is difficult to tell what it is, although chocolates might not be far out.

Two officers, two Warrant Officers and the unit's Senior NCOs pose at the bridge. The Saddler, Wheeler and Farrier sit at the front. Only the left-hand man is wearing the Overseas Volunteer badge.

ASC Drivers help the Sappers with cutting planks of wood at camp. In the background are three Daimlers and a Karrier.

The 100 yards dash, probably part of an inter-company competition during the middle weekend at annual camp. A number of family members can be seen among the military spectators in the background.

A ceremonial parade in Bridgwater, Somerset, with some forty ASC taking part in a guard of honour firing party in front of the town's Mayor and dignitaries.

The Band of the ASC in front of the Officers Mess in Woolwich, c1912. Bandmaster (WO 1) HJ Cook, who held the appointment from 1903 to 1922, sits just to the right of the bass drum, wearing a white cover on his hat.

A Lieutenant in the Army Motor Reserve (1906–1913) poses beside his shaft drive Orleans car of Belgian/British manufacture. The car (AT 427) was registered in Kingston-Upon-Hull.

Motor Volunteer Corps, c1903–1906 (see footnote 3), members at camp in the Southampton area. The gentlemen who owned cars are at the wheel, while 'lesser' gentlemen, who were later appointed as Sergeants, stand beside their motorcycles. This perceived social split caused problems.

National Motor Volunteer members, in this case the Essex Coast Section and Colchester Squadron based in Felix Hall, Kelvedon, with a selection of privately-owned cars. County units were authorized in January 1917 (see footnote 26).

HM King George V in an ASC-driven car. The driver appears to be an officer.

A line of six hired Talbot-Mors cars converted into load carriers, used by the 1st London Division ASC on training, c1913–1914.

A Dennis lorry badged to Carter Paterson & Co on training with the 1st London Division ASC, c1913–1914. There seems to be a problem with the engine, but (hopefully?) a mechanic is checking it.

1st London Division ASC again, with a Mors box car and a motorcycle, the latter probably privately owned or hired, being admired by a Second Lieutenant, while others also look on enviously.

Douglas motorcycles and riders during an inspection in Kendal, Cumbria. The General and other members of the inspecting group do not seem very interested in the men or machines.

A Model 'T' Ford ambulance, with the two ASC drivers standing on the right. Three of the four RAMC men are wearing the Territorial Force Imperial Service Badge (see footnote 27), instituted in 1908.

Regimental Police in Buller Barracks, not men to challenge on a dark night. The boy at the front might be a young trumpeter or more probably the son of one of the Regimental Policemen.

A happy work group at stables, with brushes much in evidence.

Another working group at stables. The horses are probably waiting patiently to be shoed by the Farrier Corporal (second left).

The ASC contingent marches past York Minster as part of the York Military Sunday in 1909 (see footnote 28), when all Regular and Territorial forces in York took part.

Eight GS wagons, possibly the York & Durham Company of the Northumbrian Division ASC, at annual camp. Three mounted officers are on parade.

The ASC gives a helping hand to members of the Salvation Army in what appears to be an early Commer.

A relaxed group of Territorials from the Welsh Division Transport & Supply Column at camp in Portmadoc in Wales.

'Four Men in a Boat.' Territorials of the Home Counties Division ASC on a day out at the seaside, with a Farrier at the stern and a Saddler at the bow.

Four ASC men from the Home Counties Division ASC (TF) fooling about in a village pond with a non-military wagon. The poor horse does not seem to know what to do, but then, neither do the men.

Some groups have a dog or even a goat as a mascot, but this lot has taken a donkey to their hearts. And the donkey seems happy to help, perhaps knowing it will not be eaten in the morning.

'Training Army Service Corps recruits to pass supplies across a river.' Well, the 'river' in this case is the Basingstoke Canal on the northern side of Buller Barracks in Aldershot, and the training may well have been rewarding, but there is no record of this technique ever being used by the ASC during the war.

A proud father.

An MT man with his new bride.

An HT Sergeant and his wife.

A Staff Sergeant Major and his wife.

The funeral of an ASC man on Station Road, with large crowds paying their respects, Aldershot, c1910. The main town Post Office is the striped building, top, just visible on the left side of the street.

The postcard caption, 'Funeral of the late Pte. Hunt. "A" Coy A.S.C.', is incorrect, as the funeral was in fact for Private Hunt's young son, which accounts for the single small carriage at the rear and lack of a cortege. The group is marching through Buller Barracks *en route* to the Military Cemetery. Sadly, the boy's grave no longer exists.

Men and horses of the West Riding Division Column ASC on the quayside in Douglas on the Isle of Man for their annual camp, c1910.

The ASC Woolwich football team won the Army Challenge Cup, the Army's premier sports trophy, for the first time in April 1914, beating seven Infantry or Cavalry teams to achieve this (see footnote 29).

Chapter 3: Training on the Home Front: 1914–1915

Rear view of Grove Park, London SE12, built in 1899–1902 as a workhouse (see footnote 30). In 1904 the buildings became empty and were requisitioned by the ASC in September 1914 for use as a selection and training depot for MT trades, also for the repair and issue of vehicles and the dispatch of units overseas. It became a major establishment for the training of the ASC in mechanical trades, soon to be complemented by the establishment of Osterley Park as a centre for MT training.

The main entrance to Grove Park, with two motor cycles about to depart. This view is unchanged today (2016), except that the ivy has gone and the two gaslights on top of the entrance columns are now run by electricity.

A motorcar leaves the front entrance of Grove Park on Marvels Lane, while members of the permanent staff wait for a bus. It would not be possible nowadays to push a pram down the centre of the road or indeed merely to stand there.

View inside the front entrance to Grove Park, showing a number of cars, mostly privately owned. This was an entrance for officers only, so any soldiers would have been staff car drivers or batmen.

Tented accommodation behind the main Grove Park building. The message on the back reads: 'This is the Front Part of our Camp on the road. Those big tents are where we have our meals & the others are where the Police sleep. At the back is the cookhouse.'

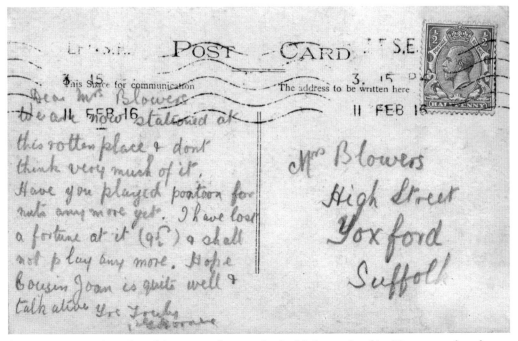

'We are now stationed at this rotten place & don't think much of it. Have you played pontoon for nuts any more yet. I have lost a fortune at it (9d) and shall not play any more. Hope Cousin Joan is quite well & talkative'. The card was sent from Grove Park to the High Street, Yoxford, Suffolk.

An LGOC instructor (see footnote 31) and the eight learners. All individuals are identified by name (Bus driver Smith, (rear) Pickford, Williams, Wilson), (front) Whittle, Armit, R.G.S., Farrier and Wilkinson).

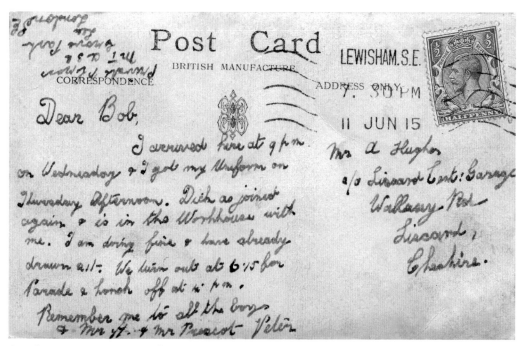

Another new recruit writes home. 'I arrived here at 9 pm on Wednesday & got my Uniform on Thursday Afternoon. Dick as joined again & is in the Workhouse with me. I am doing fine & have already drawn 21/- [21 shillings]. We turn out at 6.15 for Parade & Lunch off at 4 pm. Pte PC Moss MT ASC, Grove Park, Lee, London, SE.' Card sent to Liscard Cent. Garage, Wallassey Road, Liscard, Cheshire.

A FWD lorry with LGOC instructor and his eight men. They took it in turns through the day to drive under instruction, probably about an hour each man. Note the canvas canopy for use in inclement weather. The vehicle appears to have suffered a minor collision, damaging the left side of the radiator.

ASC lorries waiting at the junction of Spring Grove Road and London Road in Isleworth, ready to risk driving around London yet again (see footnote 32).

'"The Old and the New". MT ASC and the Chelsea Pensioner. 1915.' Unusually, six learner drivers appear with two LGOC instructors

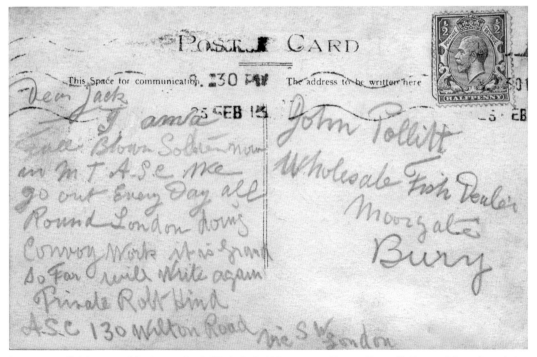

'I am a Full Blown soldier now in MT A.S.C. We go out Every Day all Round London doing Convoy Work it is grand so far will write again. Private Robt Hind A.S.C. 130 Wilton Road, SW London.' The card was posted on 25 February 1915 and sent to the Wholesale Fish Dealer in Moorgate, Bury.

'Townsend's Merry Eight on the Berlin Non-Stop', posing around their Pagefield lorry. Not much merriment visible here though.

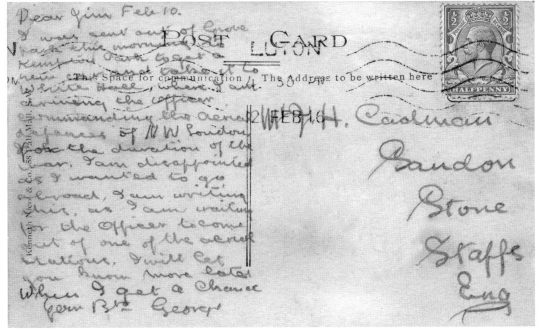

The message reads: 'I was sent out of Grove Park to Kempton Park to get a new car and take it to White Hall, where I am driving the officer commanding the aerial defences of NW London for the duration of the war. I am disappointed as I wanted to go abroad. I am writing this, as I am waiting for the officer to come out of one of the aerial stations. I will let you know more later when I get a chance.' The card was posted in Luton on 12 February 1916 and sent to Sandon, Stone, Staffordshire.

Three learner drivers this time, beside their Pierce Arrow lorry, registration number 164630. They probably needed extra training to finish the course, there being no actual driving tests in those days.

Their happy smiles reflect perhaps a successful bit of driving in their Italian-built SPA lorry, of which only small numbers were bought for use by the British Army. A '620 Coy' stencil can be seen; the unit supported the Army Postal Services, located in Regent's Park and Kensington Barracks in London.

A group of ninety-six instructors from the London General Omnibus Company (LGOC), who trained ASC driver trainees during 1915 to 1917 at Grove Park and Osterley Park, Middlesex (see footnote 33). The overwhelming majority are wearing ASC cap badges

This photograph, taken in 1916, shows the number of men in Hounslow (a thousand or more can be seen in the background) who receive instruction every day.

Five trainees out this time, with an ASC instructor (see footnote 34).

A Dennis lorry with an ASC instructor, with no canopy, probably in Hounslow (see footnotes 35 and 36).

It is unusual to see an ASC driving instructor (left-hand man, note the stylish trouser turn-ups) and only two learner drivers, both of whom are wearing cloth ASC shoulder titles.

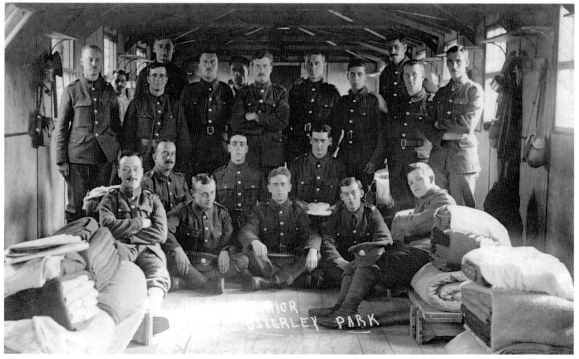

A rare picture of the interior of a hut in the Osterley Park grounds, with a small group of trainees and their glowering Corporal instructor. Note the wooden beds, which do not make comfortable seats.

Osterley Park had two mascots, dog 'Buller', named after the famous General who commanded British troops in the South African war of 1899–1902, and donkey 'Neddy'.

A 1915 card for the driver trainees to send home, showing five scenes of life in Osterley Park: 'Lining up for Drill', lines of tents with kit laid out in the open air, a crowd of men waiting to be marched away, the two mascots 'Buller' and 'Neddy', and 'MT ASC Boys at Dinner.'

A crowd of soldiers at Grove Park, relaxing before or after a parade, or perhaps a draft ready to move on.

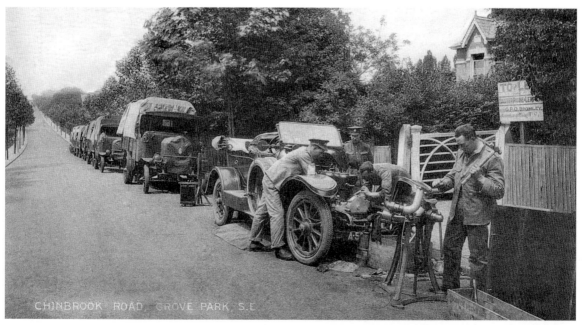

Fitters working on a London-registered car on Chinbrook Road in Grove Park on a public road, since there were no workshop facilities within the barracks. They have the cylinder head off; seen also are a portable forge (behind the car) and a mobile fitter's bench (in front of the car). Repair work with no cover must have been difficult and unpleasant during the winter months.

'HMS Dugout' in Grove Park, with a 4x4 FWD lorry with a crane to recover the no doubt numerous daily breakdowns during driver training. The officer on the Douglas motor cycle (registration GP 50), seen with his team of Fitters, wears the ribbon of the Military Cross and two wound stripes.

A Locomobile (near right) and Halley lorries are being prepared for a day's training with the learners in Kingsley Road, close to the Hounslow Town Station in 1916. Routes include Marble Arch, Hyde Park Corner, Oxford Circus and Pall Mall.

A section-worth of Napier lorries lined up, probably in the Grove Park area. With no driving instructors and bare number plates, it would appear that these are newly-issued vehicles for a unit ready to move to the West Country for work-up training before being tasked to a field force formation.

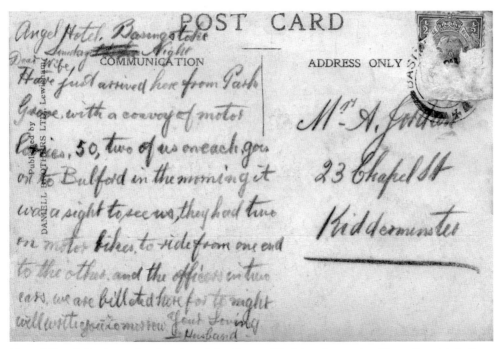

'Angel Hotel, Basingstoke, Sunday night. Dear wife, Have just arrived here from Park Grove, with a convoy of motor lorries, 50, two of us on each, goes on to Bulford in the morning it was a sight to see us, they had two on motor bikes, to ride from one end to the other, and the officers in two cars, we are billeted here for the night will write you tomorrow. Your loving husband.'

Ambulances lined up in the Grove Park area, with the officer's car and a motor cycle at the front. The two front vehicles have no number plates, so these are probably newly-issued vehicles, ready to leave.

An ASC Corporal on a new Triumph motor cycle (no number plate yet) in the Grove Park area. In the background are a Model 'T' Ford and Sunbeam ambulance.

ASC ambulances undergoing routine driver maintenance on the public roads in Grove Park. They are probably part of a unit about to depart and not vehicles used for driver training.

A Daimler 'Presented to the Grove Park Mechanical Transport Depot ASC by Past & Present Members of the Mens Mess'; however, almost in contradiction to this, 'This Lighting Set Presented By L.A.V. Co' is painted left of the rear wheel. The lighting set was no doubt useful for the Fitters, especially in the dark.

'Lieu: Lees and Staff Inspecting No 9 Coy's Lines, Osterley, 1915'.

'The Osterley Park Hairdressing and Shaving Saloon—M.T. A.S.C. 1915'. With three (empty) beer glasses on the right, extras were also available. The two brush orderlies presumably swept up the unwanted hair.

More accommodation in Osterley Park, temporary huts in this photograph. Kit arranged outside on the grass was probably a daily occurrence (so long as the weather was good).

The most popular parade in the Army: the weekly pay parade. An officer hands over the cash (which looks like a white £5.00 note), the amount is being read on the acquittance roll by the Staff Sergeant (with turn-ups on his trousers at the far end of the table), with a witness standing behind the makeshift table.

A selection of driver training vehicles outside Hounslow Bus Depot, opened in 1913, along with the LGOC instructors and ASC Fitters. Vehicles shown are Halley, Maudslay, Napier, Pierce Arrow, FWD, Belsize, Dennis, Daimler, Commer, Albion and Straker-Squire. The Duke of Cambridge pub stands in the background.

More driver training vehicles at the Hounslow Bus Depot in 1915–1916. The variety of types was in part to give drivers experience of different vehicles they would meet up with in their units, although availability from trade largely dictated what the ASC used. This was a situation that soon led to huge spares problems.

'Hounslow Garage (War Depot MT ASC 1915)'. The signs on the lamp post outside the Hounslow garage indicate the way to the Underground Hounslow Town Station.

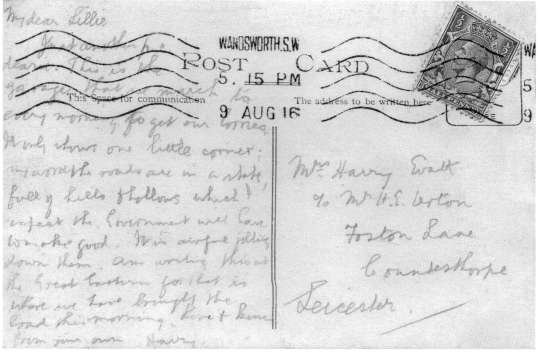

'Just another p.c. dear. This is the garage we march to every morning to get our lorries. It only shows one little corner; my word the roads are in a state, full of hills & hollows, which I expect the Government will have to make good. It is awful jolting down them. Am writing this at the Great Eastern for that is where we have brought the load this morning.'

An Austin car and Triumph motor cycle sit at the head of a convoy, with two officers and some 100 men posing all over the five lead lorries in Hounslow, perhaps at the end of training.

Lorries lined up outside the old Hounslow tram depot in 1916, ready for another day's driver training.

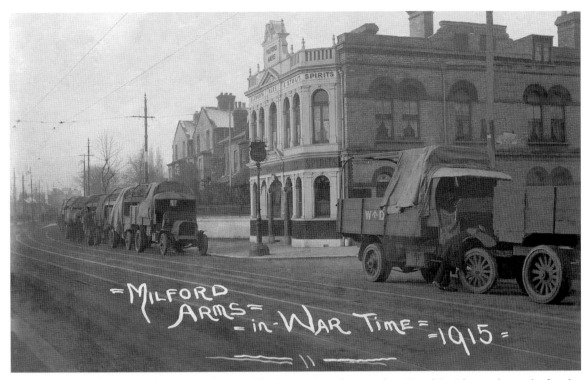

Parked up outside the mid-19th century Milford Arms on the London Road in Isleworth, ready for the driver trainees to arrive. The pub has hardly changed over the years, but parking nowadays would be impossible.

Kitchener's Knuts. 'K'nuts of 206 Coy: Park Royal: Xmas 1915' (see footnote 37).

Part of the ASC camp on Bromley Road, Catford in London. A long queue of men waits patiently outside the food tent.

Christmas dinner in 1916 at Kempton Park near Sunbury-on-Thames, Surrey, established in October 1915 as an MT Vehicle Depot. Towards the end of the war, Prime Minister Lloyd George wanted racing restarted, so the depot was moved to Slough, a hugh task.

Card sent by Pte J Townend, 180788, 704 Company, 30th MAC [Motor Ambulance Column], Grove Park, Lee, S.E.

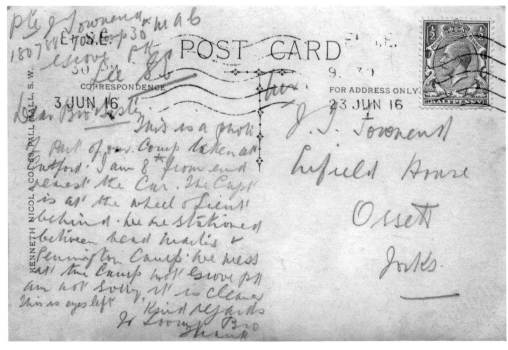

The message reads: 'This is a photo of part of our Comp [Company] taken at Catford. I am 8th from end nearest the car. The Capt is at the wheel & Lieut behind. We are stationed between headquarters and Pennington Camp. We mess at the camp not Grove Pk am not sorry, it is cleaner This is eyes left.'

Another Motor Ambulance Convoy (MAC) formed up on Inchmer Road, Catford. The nearest men are RAMC, probably medical orderlies. An MAC was an RAMC unit, with transport provided by the ASC.

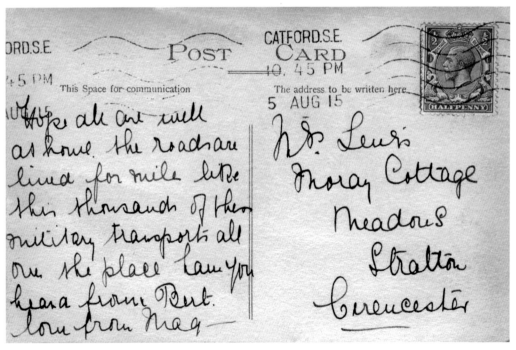

The message on the back of the card above reads: 'Hope all is well at home. the roads are lined for mile like this thousands of them military transports all over the place have you heard from Bert.'

These look like newly arrived lorries, parked on Bellingham Road, Catford (almost out in the country, all changed and built up today), with Fitters on the right perhaps carrying out initial inspections.

A line of Model 'T' Fords with Ford engine muffs on Bromley road, Catford in March 1916. The sender of the card, probably the driver of one of these ambulances, writes that he is going to Bulford the next day to be attached to an ambulance convoy. Most Model 'T's were employed in the Middle East (see footnote 38).

London omnibuses, requisitioned from the London General Omnibus Company, are lined up at Grove Park, in the process of having their peacetime livery of red and white overpainted with khaki paint.

A Locomobile omnibus drives away, leaving the others to complete their paintwork. 'MT Coy ASC' and the platoon number (in this case number 21) are stencilled on its side.

The old red and white livery of the LGOC is now a memory. Bus number 14 is visible in the centre.

Painting seems to have been completed and the scene suggests an imminent move. An admin lorry can be seen on the left, with two Triumph motor cycles, their Senior NCO riders and the platoon commander's Wolseley car add interest.

Captain Townson and the No 2 Company group at the Star & Garter Hotel in Richmond (see footnote 39).

'Blackheath Knuts'. No 2 Reserve Horse Transport Depot in Blackheath in February 1915 (see footnote 40).

An HT Lance Corporal, probably with his son or younger brother, poses at camp on a Douglas motor cycle sidecar registration number LY-2724.

132 Company: Changing of the guard in Holcombe, Somerset, a village that was buried after the devastation caused by the Black Death in the 1350–1360s. The Company became the Ammunition Sub Park for the 9th Division in 7th Corps on the Western Front.

Officers' quarters and the entrance to No 2 Centre MT ASC in 'The Camp' in the Bulford/Tidworth area on Salisbury Plain, officially entitled 'the Bulford Mobilisation and Embarkation Area', which opened in 1915.

A Dennis lorry parked outside the YMCA in 'The Camp' in Tidworth.

The tented camp of 260 Company close to Wells Cathedral in Somerset. The company became the Ammunition Park for the 16th Division on the Western Front.

260 Company on parade in front of Wells Cathedral in 1915. The photographer, Bert Phillips, was the city's resident photographer, with his premises in the city centre.

A 133 Company group in the main square in Wells on the 14th March 1915. 'Nobbler' might or might not be the civilian holding the traces in the centre, but this was evidently a successful outing.

An unidentified ASC group parading in front of Wells Cathedral in 1915 for a church parade.

Pay day for 133 Company in Wells in 1915. Two Corporals act as witnesses and a Staff Sergeant completes the acquittance rolls, while two junior officers handle the cash. Coins are visible but no banknotes.

Members of 133 Company relax during mess tin cooking on manoeuvres. The company supported the 10th and then the 14th Divisions as the Divisional Supply Column on the Western Front.

Albions of 133 Company leave Wells on a summer's day in 1915 *en route* to France, via Avonmouth. The lead lorry has 'ASC BUL' stencilled on the bonnet and 'Wells to Berlin' written in the dust on a side panel.

Major General Frederick Landon, late ASC, Inspector ASC and Quarter-Master General Services, with 134 Company in Holcombe in 1915 (he is facing the other way) (see footnote 41).

Preparation for an inspection of workshop vehicles by Major General Landon in the main square of Wells.

Eight new Douglas motor cycles of 134 Company in Wells showing sequential registration numbers, with the Officer Commanding and his Company Sergeant Major in attendance.

A smiling group in 244 Company in Holcombe, Somerset, with their LGOC B-Type lorry (see footnote 42).

A wooden-wheeled Seabrook-Standard in Holcombe of 244 Company. The letters 'AF' on the radiator indicate that antifreeze is being used in order to protect the engine in freezing weather.

'Nothing doing in iron crosses'. A winter's day in 244 Company which, in the absence of work, allows Drivers Pike and Hay and Lance Corporal Loranis (?) to build a snowman decorated with an iron cross.

244 Company leaves Holcombe for the Middle East and Egypt, via Avonmouth in 1915 (see footnote 43).

The string band of 259 Company in Wells, a fine collection of musicians.

A 'Y' type Daimler of 259 Company with no bonnet or radiator.

'Some Oven. Some Beef.' A solitary Aldershot oven is used to cook dinner in camp for men of 260 Company.

'Money for Nothing, I don't think'. Men of 260 Company, helped by local schoolchildren, whitewash the walls of a swimming pool, probably in Wells.

A full 260 Company inspection in the main square of Wells; all men have rifles, ammunition pouches and haversacks. Only three inspecting officers can be seen, so this must have been a time-consuming inspection.

'Are we downhearted. I don't think.' 260 Company men on parade again in Wells, this time with greatcoats and kitbags or blanket rolls. A unit move might be the reason.

Two lines of Peerless lorries belonging to 302 Company are parked in the High Street of Marlborough, probably in the winter of 1915–1916. Note the 3-leaf clover, the sign for supplies, on the canopies.

The ASC takes a break in Honiton, Devon (see footnote 44).

THE SNOW-CLAD COTSWOLD HILLS, AND
CHIPPING SODBURY, GLOUCESTERSHIRE.   (Dowding.)

A distant view from the clock tower of 494 Company's Thornycroft lorries, parked up on a winter's day in the 12th century town of Chipping Sodbury in the Cotswolds of Gloucestershire, where town photographer Maurice Dowding took the opportunity of recording the vehicles and men of the ASC training locally.

186.– BAND OF M.T. C° 494 A.S.C., CHIPPING SODBURY.

The Band of 494 Company in Chipping Sodbury, some standing easy and pretending to play, others standing to attention, but all ready for the Sunday church parade.

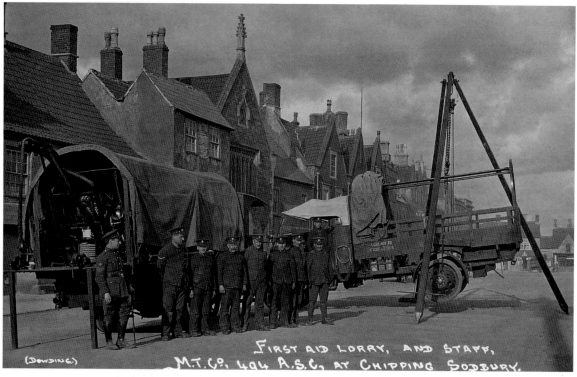

'First Aid Lorry and Staff'. Featured on the right is a heavy lift tripod with pulleys supporting a lorry, while a retractable crane to lift major assemblies can be seen on the recovery wagon on the left.

The Sunday church parade marches past their lined-up vehicles, all with radiator muffs in place, and local inhabitants and children in attendance. The unit guard on the left is presenting arms, with bayonets fixed.

494 Company tents are located next to the 13th century Church of St John the Baptist.

The entrance to the tented accommodation area of 494 Company, photographed from the church tower (see the tower's shadow bottom right). The guard tent, post room, company office, car park and workshop lorries can be seen on the left of the entrance. Top left is an NCO cadre, training to give words of command.

THE GENERAL'S OBSERVATION CAR.

A Raphael Tuck's Oilette of an imagined but not very realistic scene.

A close Shave

A despatch rider chancing it. Artist: Edgar A Holloway (1870–1941).

An ASC bakery in the field, showing freshly-cooked bread.

A Raphael Tuck's Oilette showing a steam tractor towing a 60-pounder gun.

A Holt caterpillar towing a trailer of supplies.

An ASC lorry carrying supplies in France. Artist: Edgar A Holloway.

A Tuck's Oilette depicting a sidecar
combination and an (unlikely) brigadier.

An officer and Driver ASC.
Artist: Edgar A Holloway.

The ASC MT Girl (very imaginary scene).

ASC forward ammunition supply, 1914.

A typical Laurence Colborne 'comic' card.

An overprinted Christmas card.
Artist: Laurence Colborne.

Another overprinted Christmas card
(artist not known).

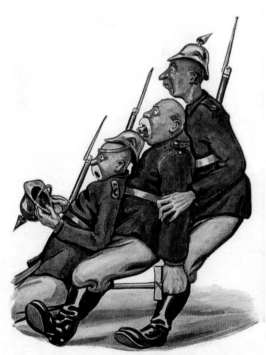

Unrealistic 'comic' card (artist not known).

An ASC staff car, with flags of the Allies.

A stylish ASC staff car, again with flags of the Allies.

A typical 'vertical' ASC silk.

A Merchant Navy 'Red Duster' with a staff car.

An Expeditionary Force Canteens silk.

A variation of the 'vertical' ASC silk.

"From One of the Army Service Corps".

"Some ASC Boy!".

"The ASC are on guard". Artist CT Howard (1865-1942).

The ASC on guard at Fleet.

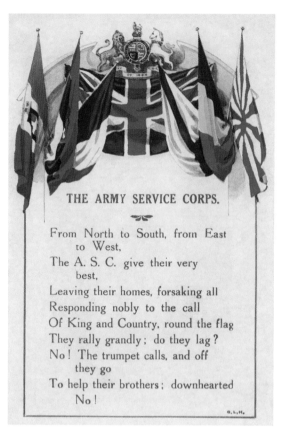

THE ARMY SERVICE CORPS.

From North to South, from East
to West,
The A. S. C. give their very
best,
Leaving their homes, forsaking all
Responding nobly to the call
Of King and Country, round the flag
They rally grandly; do they lag?
No! The trumpet calls, and off
they go
To help their brothers; downhearted
No!

"The ASC give their very best".

From One of the
ARMY
SERVICE CORPS.
Serving His
King and
Country.

I clasp your hand
in fancy
But all the while I feel
My hand is fairly
itching for
The grip that's truly real

FORGET-ME-NOT
You are always in
my Thoughts
(and Prayers)

Forget Me Not series (but no prayers!).

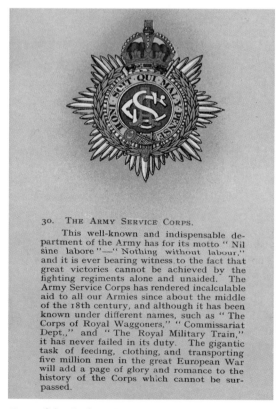

30. THE ARMY SERVICE CORPS.
This well-known and indispensable department of the Army has for its motto " Nil
sine labore "—" Nothing without labour,"
and it is ever bearing witness to the fact that
great victories cannot be achieved by the
fighting regiments alone and unaided. The
Army Service Corps has rendered incalculable
aid to all our Armies since about the middle
of the 18th century, and although it has been
known under different names, such as " The
Corps of Royal Waggoners," " Commissariat
Dept.," and " The Royal Military Train,"
it has never failed in its duty. The gigantic
task of feeding, clothing, and transporting
five million men in the great European War
will add a page of glory and romance to the
history of the Corps which cannot be sur-
passed.

One of the Badges Series
(British Photogram Co.).

ARMY SERVICE M.T. CORPS

A Grove Park card.

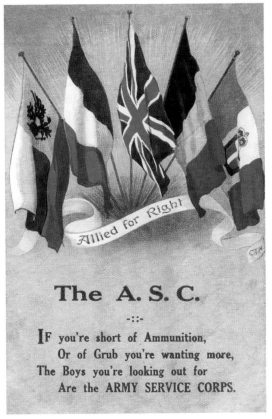

"Allied for Right". Artist:CT Howard.

"Ally Sloper's Cavalry" or "Army Slavey Corps".

A teatime note (artist Will Houghton).

Art Advertising Syndicate ASC card (artist Herbert Bryant).

THE ARMY SERVICE CORPS.

When you see a motor traction miss a lamp-post by a fraction,
  And dodge a dozen vehicles or more,
You can always bet a bob that the man who's on the job
  Is a driver in the Army Service Corps.

If you hear a waggon rumbling, and see the horses stumbling,
  Round the corner as you stand outside your door,
You can bet a crispy "fiver" that the chap who acts as driver
  Is a member of the Army Service Corps.

If you see a chap unloadin' from a ship, the stuff that's stored in
  The holds, and on the deck both aft and fore,
You can always make a bet that the fellow in a sweat
  Is a labourer in the Army Service Corps.

If you see a chap all greasy carving beef up nice and easy,
  Or a "humping" bullocks round the bloomin' store,
You can always bet a shilling, if an ox you see him killing,
  He's a butcher in the Army Service Corps.

If some dough a chap is making, or some loaves he is a-shaping,
  And he shoves 'em in the oven with his paw,
You can take your "honour bright" that the chap all dusty white
  Is a baker in the Army Service Corps.

If a chap is carting meat, or a sweeping up a street,
  Or a-scrubbing out the bloomin' office floor,
You can bet a shiny "tanner" that, judging by his manner,
  He's a clerk wot's in the Army Service Corps.

If you see a fellow lazing, or on his back just upward gazing,
  Or from his bed you hear a manly snore,
You can bet just what you like that the fellow on the "mike"
  Is an "S.R." in the Army Service Corps.

If he yells with all his might, "Advance in sections from the right,"
  "By the left, quick march," and then he says "Form fours,"
You needn't care a jot, you can bet that he has got
  The rank of sergeant in the Army Service Corps.

If you hear a fellow nagging, a-bullying or a-ragging,
  And a using language fit to break his jaw,
You can bet a quart of pop that the bloke what makes you hop
  Is a corporal in the Army Service Corps.

But if he keeps on swearing at the uniform he's wearing,
  And wishes everything to —— for evermore,
You can bet a pint of "black" that the fellow on that tack,
  Is a private in the Army Service Corps.

But when all is said and done, you'll find there ain't no fun
  In doin' just your bit to end the war ;
You can bet you've got to work, and there ain't no charnst to shirk,
  If you're in the bloomin' Army Service Corps.

By kind permission of "Ireland's Saturday Night."

A poem to bring tears to ASC eyes.

ARMY SERVICE CORPS.

✢

A.S.C. men are never still,
Day and night they work with a will.
Before the day breaks they begin,
It's late at night when they turn in.

They keep the stables clean and neat
And give their mules good food to eat,
The harness always brightly shines
Clean waggons are placed in straight lines.

Some men have no mules to attend
But with motors their time do spend
Each piece of brass is always bright,
They clean their motors every night.

The various troops on them depend,
Their many duties never end.
They carry all the things we need,
Of shot and shell they take no heed.

If the weather is wet or fine,
These noble men, they never pine,
Through wind and rain or snow and ice,
Some work at home and some in France.

So when our khaki lads you praise,
A word of thanks just try and raise
For those at home or across the sea,
God bless the men of the A.S.C.

J. F. DANIEL,
144th Field Ambulance.

7732. Williams, Printers, 231, Pentonville Rd., N.

Another patriotic ASC poem.

A hand-coloured "Driver in the ASC".

The ASC are "on the job".

"Tommy on Transport Work".

Dawn of the Army Service Corps 1902–1918.

Workshop staff of 494 Company with two workshop lorries and a stores wagon. Empty boxes (foreground left) contained stores being unpacked and placed in the stores wagons. Two new Triumph motor cycles (Army registrations 499B and 548B) can be seen.

Two officers, a Warrant Officer and NCOs of 494 Company pose on a sunny day.

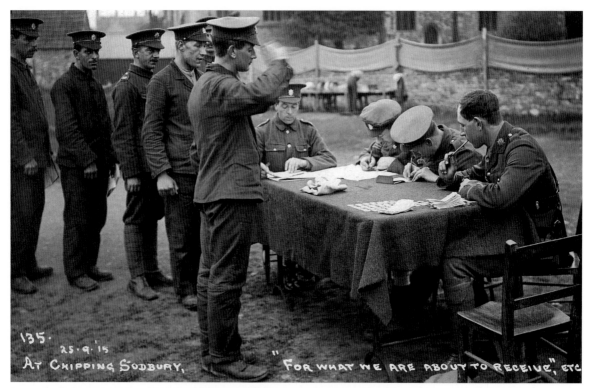

135.
25.9.'15
At Chipping Sodbury,   "For what we are about to receive," etc

Pay parade in September 1915 in Chipping Sodbury. Small piles of half-crowns or florins can be seen, and also two piles of banknotes, probably the new temporary wartime £1 and 10/= notes (authorised in 1914 and discontinued in 1928).

102.- In the A.S.C. M.T. Camp, Chipping Sodbury.

080323 Driver H Latham and others outside the 494 Company post tent, while the company runner, equipped with a smart bicycle, waits for messages.

The 494 Company tailor at work on his Singer sewing machine, helping to keep the men well turned out. His faithful terrier poses patiently. The tent's wooden base is raised off the ground.

Three tailors demonstrate their skills, one with his Singer sewing machine, one with a hot iron and the other with needle and thread.

"The two the Boys rely on – Postman and Bugler". Post collection times are on the letterbox: 10.15 am, 12 mid-day, 3.50 pm and 6.50 pm. One of the duties of the Bugler was to call the arrival of the post. (In fact, the trumpet was the official instrument for the ASC, as a mounted Corps.) There was no need to paint the stones white, as usually happened elsewhere, on the chalk lands in the Chipping Sodbury area.

Tailors in training in Aldershot in 1914. There are sixty-one students of all ages and four Sergeant instructors in the group.

Chapter 4: The Home Front: 1914–1918

This photograph probably shows the annual inspection of civilian cars registered for service with the Army in the event of war. The nearest car was registered in Bedfordshire.

Two Commer cars and a Straker-Squire, all flatbeds, have perhaps just (in 1914) been impressed into Army service. Two of them have military registration numbers and none has a civilian number, although a blank number plate can be seen on the right-hand Commer Car.

These nine Model 'T' Fords seem to be new, so had probably just been received (between July 1916 and early 1918) from the UK manufacturer in Manchester. They are probably destined for the Bulford Mobilisation & Embarkation Area to be issued in due course to newly forming MT companies, or to a London depot for issue to Home units. The lead car has a London registration number.

Wood is being chopped for the line of Aldershot ovens on the left, which must have been needed for the establishment of a very large camp. It was undoubtedly the hot work that caused the man on the left (who sent this card) to seek refreshment.

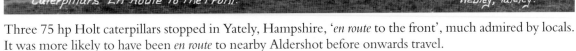

"Caterpillars" En Route To The Front.   Webley, Yateley.

Three 75 hp Holt caterpillars stopped in Yately, Hampshire, 'en route to the front', much admired by locals. It was more likely to have been en route to nearby Aldershot before onwards travel.

"Caterpillars" En Route To The Front.   Webley, Yateley

A better view of a Holt caterpillar, again in Yately, clearly newly delivered from Liverpool, where an ASC depot was established as the entry port from America.

'Changing guard' in 347 Company MT ASC in Witney, Oxfordshire.

Five members of 347 Company take their mid-day break while out on exercise, making themselves comfortable in the shade of a tree.

Drivers of 347 Company 'take tea' next to their lorries, using a variety of utensils. The company was formed in June 1915 and served in Egypt as 34 Ammunition Sub Park.

'Trench Diggers of the 347'. Four men work, sixteen men watch. Perhaps digging a trench in the Witney location of 347 Company was a punishment, with spectators, for minor offenders.

Group photograph of 704 Company at Grove Park in July 1916. Two officers, a Warrant Officer and 112 men make up the group. The company was employed as the 30th Motor Ambulance Convoy, supporting a Field Ambulance RAMC in 30 Corps on the Western Front.

The senior staff of the Supply Reserve Depot in Deptford in January 1915. The depot, which had moved from Woolwich a few weeks before the outbreak of war in 1914, was the ASC's source of supplies for the Army world-wide, holding thirty days of war reserves, among other things, of foodstuffs and forage.

A Berna lorry, registered in Bedfordshire, is used to display fresh meat, during unit training. '373 Co MT ASC' can just be seen painted on the vehicle's side, behind the hanging meat. The company was formed in June 1915 and was located in Colchester, Bedford and Hitchin.

Territorial RAMC men from the 2/4th London Field Ambulance, 2nd London Division gather around a Crossley ambulance of the ASC in Watford in April 1915. The ASC driver stands discreetly at the rear (he has seen it all before).

A French-manufactured Darracq ambulance stands outside a building, perhaps a temporary hospital, in Sunbury-on-Thames in western London.

ASC men and a Halley lorry of the 1st (Cavalry?) Division in England (see footnote 45).

Six Scottish-manufactured chain-driven Albion lorries converted to fuel tankers stand behind their seated drivers. The notice behind each vehicle states: 'Danger. No Smoking. No lights within 15 Yds'.

A bit of workshop woodwork by general fitters in the field, by the look of it making toolboxes for the stores vehicle.

An American-manufactured FWD (Four Wheel Drive) lorry in Catford, London. FWD vehicles were used to pull howitzers and medium guns of the Royal Field Artillery (while caterpillars towed the heavy guns).

A Willys Overland 1-ton lorry is well guarded, perhaps just for the photograph. Note the unusual arrangement of pneumatic tyres on the front axle and solids on the rear.

When Army accommodation was not available, soldiers were put up in billets in town; in this case twelve smart Horse Transport men are lucky.

Mr H Stephenson, Plumber & Gasfitter, with his family, provides accommodation for five ASC men, as indicated by the chalk writing on the wall. A Farrier and two, possibly three, Saddler arm badges can be seen. The Highlander in the front rank is a Gordon Highlander.

Six greys with three postilion riders at the Remount Depot in Romsey, Hampshire. On the one hand, this might be to train horses in this configuration, on the other, especially and unusually with six greys, it might be for a show demonstration.

Territorial Force at stables during annual camp. The officer and Corporal on the left are wearing the Territorial Force Imperial Service badge, instituted in 1912.

The attempt to bring a mule down at the Remount Depot in Romsey, Hampshire appears to be in difficulties.

BOYS OF THE REMOUNT DEPOT, SOPWELL, St ALBANS.

'Boys of the Remount Depôt, Sopwell, St Albans' in Hertfordshire. The star is a young boy wearing an ASC cap badge (front centre), almost certainly the son of one of the ASC members of the Depot staff.

A well-used GS wagon pulled by four mules, which are perhaps getting used to anti-insect headbands before they move to the Middle East with the sun topi-wearing riders.

A GS wagon carrying camp stores. Of interest in the background is wooden flooring for accommodation tents being manhandled onto a GS wagon.

Eighteen members of the Women's Legion in 613 Company in Liverpool (see footnote 46).

A handsome young officer explains to members of the Women's Legion how the gearbox works.

Members of 60 Field Bakery relax during the mealtime in barracks. One man is swanking with a box of Nut Milk Chocolate.

Two Senior NCOs, a Corporal and four Drivers are probably part of the night guard at Grove Park. The slightly untidy barrack room indicates that they are members of the Permanent Staff, checking their weapons before guard mounting. Note Standing Orders are pinned on the wall in the background.

Two Model 'T' Ford ambulances at Grove Park, presented by the Queenswood School, Clapham Park in south west London. After the Retreat from Mons in 1914, it became clear that, essentially due to horse fatigue, horse-drawn ambulances had to be replaced by motorized vehicles, so a worldwide appeal was made for funds to provide ambulances for the Army in the field. The response from around the world was remarkable (see footnote 47).

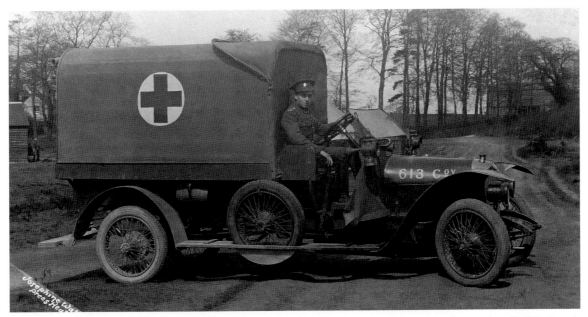

A Crossley tender used as an ambulance in 613 Company located in Prees Heath, south of Whitchurch in Shropshire. It was one of the fastest vehicles in the Army, with a top speed of 55 mph. On the unit's formation in 1916, there were twenty-one ambulances on strength, but this number increased to ninety-seven by the time the company was renumbered in 1922.

A Straker-Squire converted as a passenger-carrying lorry takes nurses from the convent to the 2nd Eastern Military Hospital in Brighton.

A Wolseley ambulance, 'County of Fife No 2', with the Edinburgh registration number S-4880 donated to the Scottish Branch of the British Red Cross Society, stands beside the road on a damp day.

A Daimler bus transports nurses to work.

The Corporal is responsible for training the thirteen women in the art of staff car driving. His slightly sickly grin suggests he might be nervous about what his wife will say when she sees this photograph.

Seven Red Cross drivers wear leather greatcoats for outside winter work on their ambulances, a convoy of which was presented by British Brewers. Note the petrol cans and funnel beside them.

Two Darracq ambulances donated by Canada wait outside the gates of Crownhill Hospital in Plymouth.

A Model 'T' Ford with the simple but very effective dedication "From Grimsby Folk to Grimsby Men".

ASC ambulance drivers support injured Indian soldiers. Two Indian Cavalry and two Infantry Divisions arrived in France only weeks after war was declared in August 1914. Sadly the winter weather and other considerations militated against them and they were moved to the Middle Eastern theatre, having suffered a total of 90,000 casualties.

A rehearsal for loading stretcher cases into ambulances during a Territorial Force exercise, observed by four officers.

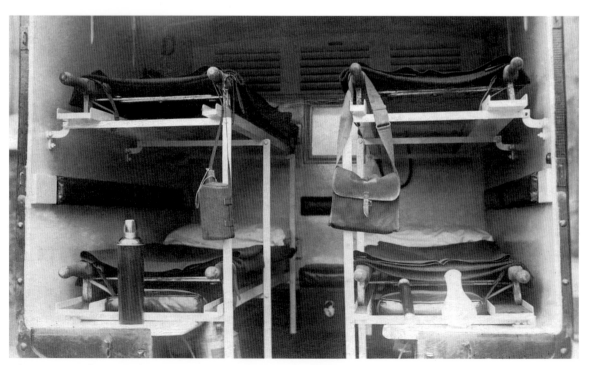

The interior of an ambulance presented by the Schools of Barrow.

Two Model 'T' Fords with an ambulance body conversion in a West Country town. The nearest one has 'Bulford 3066' stencilled on the bonnet, indicating it is on loan from Bulford stocks, to be handed back at the end of work-up training. Sometimes called 'Tin Lizzies', many Model 'T's were used with great success by the Army, particularly in Mesopotamia and Palestine.

A newly issued Model 'T' Ford ambulance, proudly showing off its quilted Ford radiator muff. The photograph was almost certainly taken in the Osterley Park/Hounslow area.

Four ASC men, real 'Kitchener's Knuts', relax in the sun at camp, with a bottle or two of ale and a plate of sausages. Men of Field Marshal Kitchener's New Armies liked to call themselves 'Knuts'.

An MT Sergeant poses on a new Triumph motor cycle registration number 537-B, probably having displaced the Lance Corporal alongside him for the photograph. Motor cycle riders do not normally wear bayonets.

After the first use of gas in warfare during the First Battle of Ypres in April 1915, the Army introduced gasmasks. This photograph shows six men being instructed in their use, somewhere in England.

Sergeants Bell and Cotter of 290 Company display their kitbags marked with their names and the three-legged Manx sign of their unit. 290 Company was the No 3 Company of the 37th Division (see footnote 48) on the Western Front from 1915 to 1919.

The Warrant Officer's dog enjoys its five minutes of fame. (Crowns on the lower arm denote Warrant Officers.)

A 1912 Austin open tourer staff car, spick & span but far from new. Note the crank handle, which was necessary to start the engine, sometimes a risky business.

Eight men enjoy, if only passingly, another open tourer staff car. Note the piles of spare tyres on the right.

Yet another open tourer, a Wolseley on this occasion. The anchor sign of the 63rd (Naval) Division can clearly be seen, left of the military registration number, M-14980. The arrow in the registration number on the bonnet indicates that the vehicle belonged to the Army.

TADWORTH. 1915.

Men of the 3rd London Mounted Brigade ASC acting the fool at camp in 1915 at Tadworth, near Epsom, Surrey.

"Weekly output of Service Wagons from Thornycroft Works, Basingstoke."   May, 1915

'Weekly output of Service Wagons from Thornycroft Works, Basingstoke. May 1915.' Eighteen Thornycroft lorries can be counted in this line. The Army used some 5,000 Thornycroft lorries during the war, most of which were the 'J' Type.

The Workshop officer from 689 Company and his three Senior NCOs pose on the open side of the chain-driven workshop machinery lorry. Visible in the lorry are a lathe, workshop bench, vertical drilling pillar and a generator.

'Our Flying Corps. May Fly Aeroplane. Praps Engine'. Workshop staff pose in front of their workshop and stores lorries, clearly have time on their hands. Work on the bare chassis of a car (Model 'T' Ford?) has been interrupted, not that the head of a pick helve will help very much.

Anti-aircraft guns ('Archies') carried by two Thornycrofts, with a subsidy Wolseley, and a Douglas motor cycle (registration no C25587). The ASC drivers of all the lorries sit resolutely in their open cabs, while the Corporal on the Douglas is also ASC. These men, except the ASC members, are all Royal Artillery, and comprise the gun crew for the 'Archies'.

Two 'J' Thornycrofts at firing camp, but the absence of sea visible in the distance would indicate only blanks are being used at an inland location. The number of men round each gun would appear to be excessive, even allowing for the surveyors (or photographers?) on the right. The dog in the foreground has seen it all before.

A Crossley boxcar 'On Duty' is flanked by two Triumph motor cycles on a muddy day. Note the different tread patterns on the boxcar. Few Crossleys were to be found in Army service, most being issued to the Royal Flying Corps.

A pre-war CB Daimler, probably requisitioned, provides a lift for a group of General Service-badged soldiers, also a lady hidden in the cab's shadows. Hmm! Note the 'Load not to exceed 2 tons' on the scuttle.

Would-be tennis players in uniform pose beside the tennis court. There was not much opportunity to play sport in those days, other than football.

Five golfing soldiers, an uncommon sight at camp. 'ASC Golf Club' is a bit of an exaggeration, since there was no Corps Golf Club then.

The football team of 51 Squadron ASC, located in Redhill, Surrey, having formed in May 1915. Only Remount units in the ASC used the term 'Squadron' as part of the Remount organization; there was a separate 51 (MT) Company in the Corps Order of Battle.

With six men at one end and seven on the other, it is not really an equal or genuine attempt at tug- of-war, especially as the rope is so thin that it is likely to break. Soldiers will be soldiers!

A stylish studio photograph.

A Saddler Staff Sergeant in the 34th Division.

Nothing like a restful day by the seaside.

Or sitting comfortably on a rattan chair.

Six Triumph motor cycles, one with a sidecar, and riders pose in front of a Thornycroft (?) and an admiring crowd.

The 'Iron Rations Orchestra & Concert Party', including seven pierrots (see footnote 49), illustrate what a small unit can do to entertain their men and other units, with support from the Officer Commanding.

Cookery School: The instructors in this photograph were ASC, but a number of Rifle Brigade and Fusilier cap badges can be seen among the students. Three demonstration ovens can be seen. (See footnote 50.)

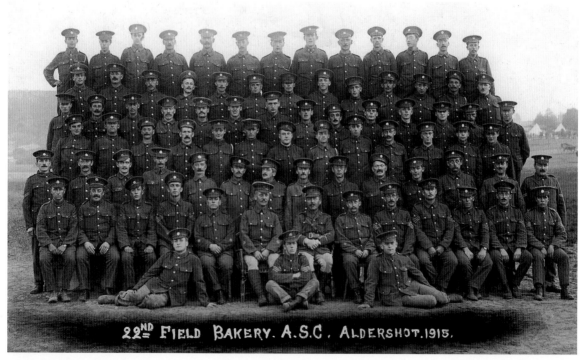

22 Field Bakery in Aldershot in 1915. The total of eighty-three men shown consists of one officer, three Warrant Officers and seventy-nine other ranks. This Field Bakery supported the 22nd Division on the Western Front and in Salonika.

Five 75 h.p. Caterpillar tractors take a break, possibly in Taunton, Somerset. They were named 'Johnnie Walker', 'Going Strong', 'Dad & Little Willie' and 'Kaiser Hearse'. The main task of the caterpillar fleet was to tow the heavy guns of the Royal Artillery, but they were used in many other roles.

The crew of a Lion Class Fowler provides support to local farmers. In this photograph, the Fowler's engine is providing power to the baling and threshing machine at harvest time.

Several Fowler steam engines, visible in an interesting photograph, appear to be moving equipment for harvesting hay. On the right, a baling machine under a canvas cover, a workman's mobile hut and another baling machine can be seen being towed by a Fowler, followed similarly by another. ASC men up to the rank of Warrant Officer and members of the Women's Forage Corps (see footnote 51) line the road.

A Clayton steamer carrying wood, probably working for the Canadian Forestry teams in Abergavenny or Penrith. A Saddler Corporal, a Horse Transport man and a Driver also pose for the photographer.

A Section's-worth of Peerless lorries and drivers from 343 Company, with their bonnets open for maintenance. The nearest vehicle has 'BUL 6970' stencilled on the bonnet, indicating that it is on loan from the Bulford pool of vehicles.

Two Sergeants pose with a Corporal and driver beside an Albion. The steps at the back probably indicate it is being used as a stores vehicle. The unit sign (between the two left-hand men) is that of the 29th Division Ammunition Park.

A Foden Thresh Disinfector (see footnote 52).

The doors of the disinfector are open, with laundry being exchanged. The laundry shown in the basket in the foreground is more likely to belong to the women in the background than to the soldiers.

'School of Destruction' fitters of the ASC were keen to extend their repair capability beyond ordinary MT vehicles, in this case a heavily modified Model 'T' Ford. Never a dull day, if you have time to spare.

Australian ASC Peerless lorries at Broadlands, Romsey, in Hampshire, the first Australian unit to arrive in England.

The band of 264 Company in Caversham in 1915, on the north side of Reading. The company was formed in March 1915 as 56 Ammunition Sub Park to support the 56th Division on the Western Front.

The cooks of 73 Company on 25 September 1914, with potato peelers at work on the right. The cooking pots were used to cook and distribute the beef stew and potatoes.

A 'Lion' Foster steam engine stands between two Model 'T' Ford ambulances, with a Sergeant posing on a Triumph motor cycle in Wareham, Dorset.

The Band of the ASC in khaki. In addition to the Commanding Officer, his Adjutant and the Bandmaster, Warrant Officer HJ Cook in No 1 Dress, there are forty-nine musicians in the group, which was almost certainly photographed in Buller Barracks, Aldershot, where they were normally based.

Two Daimlers on duty with the Royal Engineers distributing Royal Mail to Army units. The group in the middle are Sappers, with the ASC drivers leaning possessively against their vehicles.

One hundred–and–two ASC Wheelers in Woolwich in October 1916. The Wheeler's trade badge can be seen on most uniforms, so course personnel and Permanent Staff together appear here.

'Officers servants out on the spree' in the Daimler. Six of them were officers' batmen, a very sought after job compared with many others. Their duties involved looking after their officers' uniforms and turnout.

Pierrots of the ASC Discharge Depot in Catterick, Yorkshire in 1918. Major JS Iredell, the Officer Commanding, sits centre front. Many units created their own Pierrot troupes.

A doggy Happy Christmas.

Lead me to the war.

'L/Cpl Lowe MM, Despatch Rider'.

Ypres Cathedral in ruins.

An LGOC armoured car, probably in Catford, London, seemingly used for training ASC drivers posted to an armoured car unit. In 1915, 322 Company was equipped with four armoured cars and trained by Sir John Willoughby for service in East Africa – this is possibly one of those four.

An armoured Rolls Royce car in muddy conditions, location unknown. What is probably a block of concrete on the flatbed indicates this is another training vehicle in England.

978 Company's Carpenters' Shop in Claydon, Suffolk (see footnote 53).

The Erecting Shop of 978 Company, showing vehicles awaiting the replacement of their major assemblies. Just right of centre is a hand-operated mobile crane for lifting repaired engines.

The Blacksmiths' Shop in 978 Company.

The Engine Shop in 978 Company, with two engines being worked on in the foreground. The company was responsible for 1,100 vehicles in its area.

The photograph shows Scottish Blacksmiths of 136 Company, proud of their Scottish flag and bagpipes. The Company was formed in January 1915 and supported the 37th Division on the Western Front.

Two workshop vehicles side-by-side with their staff in the London area, with the side screens open.

Tack for the horses is laid out next to the stables, probably to be checked on arrival or departure during training at camp.

Farriers deal with a fractious mule by securing it in a wooden frame. Twelve people present would have been 'over the top' for such a task, so this is probably a demonstration for new Farriers.

Wheelers stand behind parts of a dismounted GS wagon on which they are working.

Weighing chopped wood at camp. An Aldershot oven requires 150 lbs a day to achieve its target.

'A double event. Haircut and Shaving.' Soldiers will have their fun, especially if Bert Phillip from Wells is around. A rubbish disposal wagon and trailer would seem to provide a suitable background.

There is nothing like a broken-down vehicle to attract attention, and no doubt helpful advice, for this impressed Maudslay flatbed, registration number CH-1058 from Derbyshire.

This Wiltshire-registered (AM-6129) Belsize lorry stands outside Christ Church in north London. With no unit identification marks, it is probably a training vehicle based in Osterley Park. The Army used few vehicles of this marque.

A group of Drivers gather round their Leyland for a relaxed, happy snap to send home; one Driver even plays a ukulele-type instrument.

A line of Hallfords in a field location in the south of England, with drivers relaxing while performing periodic vehicle maintenance under the eye of a Corporal.

A Hallford belonging to 623 Company, formed in January 1916 and based in London to provide support to units requiring assistance when the railways were involved.

On guard at Christmas.

A scrubbing brush in the cheese.

'They shall not pass!'

'I'd hit you if you were shorter'.

Ready for war?

Lightly equipped.

A good one for mum.

The new rifle holster.

Two Drivers pose with a group of Sergeants and a child, with a somewhat overloaded lorry. The Warrant Officer stands beside his Douglas motor cycle BE2900, registered in Lincolnshire.

Blankets wrapped up neatly inside their groundsheets will keep members of this guard warm at night. Posing in front of the company's Peerless lorries will make a good photo to send to the lads back home.

ASC men participate in the War Bonds campaign in Liverpool with camouflaged ASC Holt caterpillars, which pulled the 60-pounder guns. The equestrian statue of Queen Victoria can be seen top right.

Five German vehicles which had been returned after the war for trials in Buller Barracks, Aldershot. Their eventual fate is not known.

Wounded soldiers pose outside their local YMCA canteen, including two seated ASC men on the right. ASC casualties in the war were 280 officers and 8,187 men killed and about the same number wounded.

An ASC-driven ambulance, probably in London at celebrations welcoming the Armistice in November 1918.

Chapter 5: The Western Front: 1914–1918

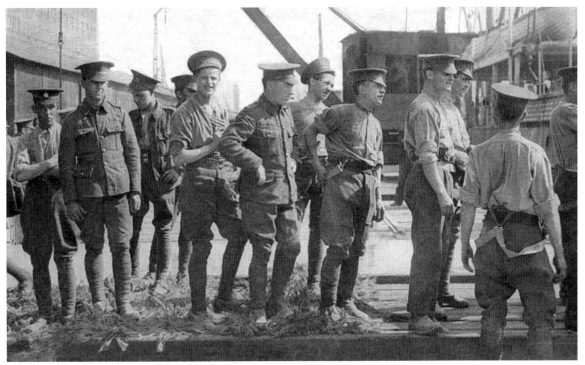

ASC Horse Transport men help to unload horses from a ship, probably in le Havre in August 1914.

Supply lorries take a break in Albert on the Somme, August 1914. As ever, the locals are curious.

More Supply vehicles appear and the locals are keen to engage with the soldiers.

Cars belonging to a formation HQ stopped in Montdidier on the Somme. The Rolls Royce displaying an Automobile Association badge was undoubtedly a requisitioned car.

Vehicles on the way to the front, including a Dennis charabanc converted as a flatbed. The Lancia car on the right was probably not a requisitioned vehicle, but it would have been a nice runabout for a keen motorist.

Officers of 56 Company, 4th Divisional Train, take tea during the retreat from Mons (see footnote 54).

Men and vehicles of a Supply convoy in France. Note the Heath-Robinson wooden frame behind the front driver, which would not have lasted long when used. The requisitioned van on the right has a Gloucestershire registration (DG-499).

A lorry full of HT men, with some MT men standing beside the lorry in Nantes on the River Loire, along with three French soldiers and three civilians.

More wood is needed to cook the dinner. Two work while the rest just watch, nothing new.

Aldershot ovens in use to bake bread in Boulogne. They appear to be set up in the town.

A bread store in Boulogne. The sacks of loaves are probably about to be issued to units.

Farriers at work in le Mans, probably at a temporary overnight location.

Two GS wagons early in 1914. It was unusual to have two men on the box in addition to the two postilions and it was not long before two horses only were used for GS wagons with a team of two men.

An Indian Supply & Transport Corps (STC) GS wagon with Sikh riders in France, c1914 (see footnote 55).

Unloading a Supply train in le Mans. Onward transport has yet to come.

Wounded arrive at a medical location in Amiens. The horsed ambulance appears to be a converted GS wagon, probably due to the shortage of ambulances in the early days of the war, before motorised ambulances arrived in France.

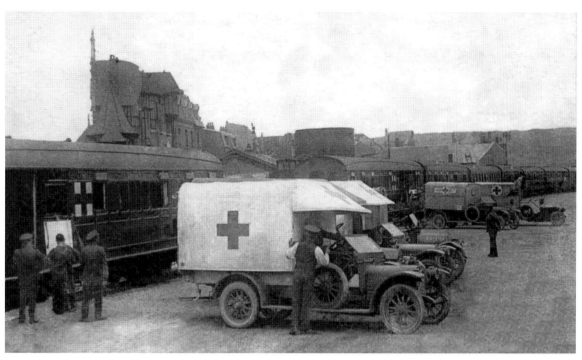

Sunbeam ambulances deliver the wounded to an ambulance train in le Tréport railway station.

London omnibuses, many full of soldiers, in the market square of Béthune. Various GS wagons and ambulances also in view suggest this is an early photograph after deployment in 1914.

A line of full London omnibuses facing east in the main square in Poperinge, Belgium, probably in September 1914.

A Daimler in the livery of the Metropolitan Electric Tramways (MET) in the city centre of Bruges in Belgium, having been used by the 63rd (Royal Naval) Division and captured by the German Army in 1914.

13. - GUERRE EUROPÉENNE 1914. — Un camion de ravitaillement
ARMY SERVICE CORPS MOTOR WAGON

A Leyland 3-ton S2 of the type bought for trials by the War Office, c1911–1912. The number plate AA-2403 was registered in Southampton. The canopy seems to be somewhat voluminous and unsafe.

A Daimler and a GS wagon manage to provide a stable base for seventy-seven men and six French family members to pose together, an impressive postcard to send home.

BRITISH CONVOYS ON THE SOMME.

Lines of GS wagons and a lorry block the roads on the Somme in 1914. 'Red Star' convoys as used in the Second World War were certainly not possible here.

Guerre Mondiale 1914-18
LE QUESNOY – Convoi de Prisonniers allemands

édit. Hautmont

A convoy of GS wagons carrying German prisoners–of–war in le Quesnoy. The spare wagon wheels indicate this photograph was taken in 1914, perhaps just before the time the German Army attacked and occupied the town. The New Zealanders liberated the town in November 1918.

Rolls Royce staff car registration M1728, with three spare tyres and possibly blackout headlights. The War Office initially requisitioned thirty-six Rolls Royce cars for the most senior of commanders in the Army. Their Majesties The King and Queen later used this Rolls Royce during a visit to the Western Front.

A Daimler staff car, registration M14410, of the type used by senior officers in the Army.

An unusual requisitioned Daimler charabanc in France. As ever, the British soldier's humour is applied in chalk: 'Non Stop Run', 'Are we downhearted. NO' and 'Via France to Berlin'. A mixture of people adds to the scene: four ASC Horse Transport men, five French soldiers, an old man, (probably) his two grandchildren as well as several ASC MT men.

A Garrett tractor in France in 1918. The tin-hatted man playing a squeezebox is probably enjoying the warmth of the chimney before it goes cold.

A requisitioned Model BT Leyland used to carrying parcels but now carries Army supplies (see footnote 56).

A Red Cross Rolls Royce, modified as an ambulance, still retaining its London registration (LF–7478) and Automobile Association badge in addition to its Army registration, visits a makeshift Red Cross workshop.

An interesting photograph of three Dennis Stevens lorries, a 1917 Model 'T' Ford and a Triumph motor cycle in France. What is unusual is that the two outside lorries have different camouflaged canopies, a late introduction on the Western Front, while the centre lorry has glossy paint applied. Hidden by the canopies are a searchlight and anti-aircraft gun (an 'Archie').

A camouflaged 'Archie' of the Royal Garrison Artillery and a camouflaged Peerless lorry of the ASC.

A subsidy Dennis 'A' Type lined up with others in a French market square, probably in 1914.

An AEC (Associated Equipment Company) 'Y' Type lorry parked up in the same town in France as the above Dennis. The chains dangling down on the side were to improve wheel grip in snowy or muddy conditions.

A Swiss Saurer lorry (over)loaded with hay for the horses. At least this hay was freshly cut from a French farm, compared with the less desirable compressed hay sent from the Deptford Supply Depot in England.

Two Corporals seem to have the time to play a game of draughts. Both have overseas service stripes, suggesting the photograph was taken later in the war, without shot and shell disturbing their concentration.

An example perhaps of good Anglo-French relations during the war. A number of ASC men, from HT as well as MT units, pose in front of a clearly successful bistro with French police and civilians.

HRH Princess Mary's Christmas box (see footnote 57).

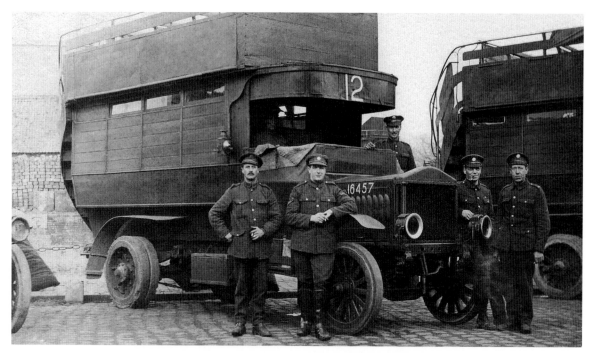

A Locomobile lorry of 405 Company is fitted with an LGOC B-Type bus body.

London busmen of D Section [Platoon] of 90 Company (the 1st Auxiliary Omnibus Company).

A well-maintained Locomobile omnibus with its driver, accompanied by a Triumph motor cycle and rider. The four Overseas Service stripes of the standing man indicate this is a 1918 photograph.

BRITISH TROOPS WHO DROVE THE HUNS OUT OF LESBEOUFS.

Infantry enjoy a lift on a column of charabancs (see footnote 58).

Two Straker-Squires and a Wolseley are stopped on the road, having collected timber with the help of Indian labourers. The scene is difficult to place, but could be either southern France or Italy.

Workshop staff of 736 Company (40th Auxiliary Steam & Petrol Company), which was formed in July 1916 to support Line of Communication units on the Western Front. The workshop commander and his Staff Sergeant both wear three overseas service stripes and five of the group appear to be wearing the ribbon of the 1914–1915 star, so this photograph was probably taken c1918.

Foster and Fowler steam engines in the 2nd ASC Workshop in Rouen. The left-hand Foster was registered in Lincoln (FE-1296) and still has 'Radfield & Sons' stencilled on the canopy.

Two Clayton steamers looking smart in the muddy conditions. 934 Company ASC (67th Auxiliary (Steam) Company) supported the Assistant Director Roads, Second Army, on the Western Front.

An Australian Army workshop in Cairo, possibly in Gamrah, with a variety of ambulances on both sides, some under repair. The ambulance pulled out of line on the left is a Napier.

A Heavy Repair Workshop in Rouen, formed in January 1917, operated by 899 Company, with skilled labour provided by German prisoners of war. The sign hanging in the centre of the Inspection & Repair Bay reads "Smoking Forbidden. Rauchen Verboten". Note the internal railway track.

A Daimler lorry used temporarily for specific battles to carry walking wounded, with the two drivers standing at the front and a medical orderly at the back. There is a unit sign on the scuttle, but the oblique angle makes identification difficult.

A Daimler ambulance donated by Thanet has seen better days,. The sand on which the ambulance is standing suggests a coastal location in France.

A Fiat ambulance from the 7th Cavalry Brigade, 3rd Cavalry Division in France. It is unusual to see 'OHMS' on the windscreen. Note the 'good luck' horseshoe above the windscreen, easy to obtain in a Cavalry Division.

A Talbot ambulance donated by 'The Association of Saint Peter's Collegians South Australia for Service with the British Army in the Field' in France (see footnote 59).

An Argyll ambulance named 'Mauldslie' of the Scottish Branch of the British Red Cross Society, somewhere in France. Argyll was arguably the best-known Scottish motoring manufacturer.

Ambulances in a forward area, probably at a Forward Field Dressing Station. This photograph was used in the 'Daily Mail' set of postcards.

A Locomobile fitted with a water tank in 718 Company, the 2nd Water Tank Company (see footnote 60).

Two Maudslays take a break. Note the unusual (and temporary?) mascot on the bonnet of the front lorry and the probability that the rear lorry has no brakes, so has to park against the front lorry to stop it moving.

A Holt 75 hp caterpillar on the tractor park, showing several in the background with their canvas protective screens rolled down, an unusual sight.

A Holt driver showing off with a "pretend" wheelie, probably in France judging by the building in the background. Just to the right of the right-hand soldier can be seen the unit sign of 77th Siege Battery Ammunition Column.

A Daimler in support of the Royal Engineers road services. Above the driver's cab can be seen the cut-out sign, which appears to be the barbell sign of the 3rd Canadian Division.

GS wagons of New Zealand Division units collect rations at the Divisional rations dump.

A Leyland of the 51st (Highland) Division ASC stands outside a French bistro, where the drivers have clearly stopped for refreshment. The Highland Division 'HD' sign can be seen above the driver's cab.

A total of thirty-one men make up this ASC unit band (with a little outside help, in the form of four members of the Royal Artillery, including the Bandmaster). Four officers can be seen, also a French interpreter, in the front row.

A Daimler tests out the replacement wooden road laid by New Zealand Pioneers after the advance in 1918.

A Karrier WDS in France. Unusually a water tank and pump can just be seen beside the two German prisoners-of-war in the back.

Two Leylands blocking the road in France, presumably to set up a group photograph. To add a typical bit of soldier humour, the sign reads, 'Leyland Tea and Sugar Testers'. Inside one cab is also visible the chalked words 'Mon Abri' ('My Shelter' or even 'My Hole').

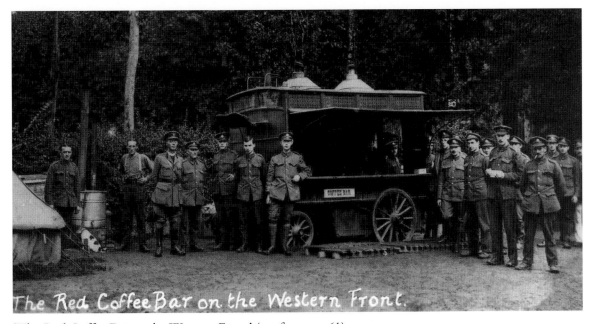

'The Red Coffee Bar on the Western Front' (see footnote 61).

One of the teams with their projectors (from 339 Company in this case – see the elephant sign) that showed films to units within a Division on the Western Front during the war.

Musicians of the 31st Division MT Company (527 Company), as the cinema staff, supporting film shows around the Division at Christmas time 1918.

Chapter 6: Overseas Theatres: 1914–1919

Germany. Entry of the first British troops in Cologne on 7 January 1919, led by a Cavalry regiment.

Germany. Among the first British troops crossing the bridge in Cologne on 7 January 1919 are three RASC Peerless lorries, followed by a number of GS wagons. Judging by the pedestrians on the left side, normal life seems to be continuing for the German populace. (The ASC had been granted the title 'Royal' on 27 November 1918.)

Germany. RASC cars and ambulances parked on the square opposite the HQ of the British Army of Occupation in Cologne in 1919, in the Excelsior Hotel on the left. Out of sight on the right is the Cologne cathedral. Officers and soldiers walk normally among the German inhabitants. The entrance to the main railway station can be seen at the top right.

Germany. A different view of the square outside Cologne cathedral, with its steps visible on the right.

Germany. Two staff car drivers wait for their officers in Cologne, leaning possessively against a Wolseley and a Vauxhall. The Bank for Trade and Industry stands in the background on the right.

Germany. More staff car drivers waiting in Cologne, three Wolseleys and a Model 'T' Ford this time.

Germany. View of Cologne from the east, showing the bridge over which the first British troops entered the city. The MT yard of an RASC unit can also be seen in the bottom left corner.

Germany. A souvenir postcard from Cologne in 1919, showing the cathedral, the Rhine Bridge and the paddle steamer 'Rheinland'. The five Horse Transport Drivers are wearing RASC shoulder titles and cap badges.

Germany. View of a well-stocked Expeditionary Force Canteen store in Cologne.

Germany. GS wagons unload fresh meat from rail wagons in Cologne. Note the cloth draped over the body of the GS wagon in the centre of the photograph to wrap the meat for the journey to the Supply Depot, good hygiene practice in those days.

Germany. '2 and 34 Road Sections RASC M.T. Bonn. Germany. 1919'. A Lieutenant sits on his Douglas motor cycle, with one Sergeant and forty-four men in what could be a brewery yard.

Germany. A souvenir postcard shows the Rhine Bridge in Bonn, also an RASC Horse Transport Driver.

Germany A Holt caterpillar in July 1919 in Bonn, with workshop Fitters working on one of the tracks. The swastika, a mystical symbol from ancient times, seen on the radiator of the second caterpillar, was a unit sign until the company was disbanded after the war, but understandably it has not been used since then.

Germany. One thing that is "Indispensible" in the Army is fatigues, in this case peeling potatoes in Cologne.

Germany. Workshop members of the 20th Motor Ambulance Convoy (638 Company) in Cologne.

Germany. Two Triumph motor cycles, one a sidecar version, registration number C9010, ridden by two smart Drivers in Cologne.

Germany. An RASC contingent of Horse Transport and MT groups, take part in a church parade in Cologne. Note the bandoliers are reversed and on the right shoulder to provide space on the left shoulder for rifles.

Germany. A German lorry, an Erhardt, in the ASC workshop in Cologne. The adjustable snowplough on which the Lance Corporal is standing is remarkable for the time, as is the rear suspension with four wheels, perhaps catering for a lorry-mounted anti-aircraft gun.

Germany. Number 4 Section of 1132 Company gathers together at Christmas 1918 for a group photograph in Düren, near Cologne. The company was formed only in October 1918 as the 18th Reserve MT Company.

Germany. Number 4 Company of the 34th Divisional Train RASC, located in February 1919 in Siegburg.

Germany. General view of the London Division's Horse Show in Overath, east of Cologne, in 1919. Two display rings are in use, with Royal Artillery limbers being judged on the left and a number of GS wagons in the right-hand ring. The ASC always did well in the GS wagon competitions.

Germany. A Sergeants' Mess group in Cologne in 1919. All visible Overseas Service stripes reflect a minimum of four years service abroad, but it is strange that no medal ribbons are to be seen.

Germany. A Dennis Stevens lorry outside the Rheinhotel Dreesen near Bonn (see footnote 62).

Germany. Buller Barracks, the RASC barracks, in Wiesbaden, the location of the HQ of the British Army of the Rhine in 1925 until the withdrawal of all occupation forces in 1930. British troops finally left Cologne in 1926.

Chapter 7: Other Theatres of War

Egypt. Four ASC men, one pyramid and a sphinx. There is probably a perfectly simple reason why one of the men is riding a white mule.

Egypt. Gabbari Camp in Alexandria on the north coast of Egypt, showing GS wagons, accommodation tents and what are probably vehicle bays.

North West Frontier of India. Ambulances of the 28th Motor Ambulance Convoy (630 Company), almost certainly in the Khyber Pass. The Company had been formed in January 1916, serving in Bangalore and Rawalpindi.

North West Frontier of India. ASC lorries transporting sacks of supplies can be seen winding round the roads of the Khyber Pass.

Italy. Number 2 ASC Horse Transport & Supply Depot at Arquata, formed by 1046 Company in November 1917, showing Daimler lorries on the left and GS wagons on the right (loaded with manure?). The message on the postcard says, 'The Rest Camp is just off the right of the post card. The horses are stabled in the large building with chimney attached. Those hills at the back are covered with grape vines.'

Italy. Stores from Canada are being unloaded from ASC lorries, with two Italian Army men in attendance.

Italy. Roads in the forward areas used by the ASC were in range and under observation by Austrian guns in the mountains, so certain lengths of road were hidden from view by this home-made camouflage netting.

Mesopotamia. There were few if any roads in 'Mespot' (as the country was colloquially known to the soldiers) and the River Tigris was extensively used for movement, especially of supplies. Barges appear to be used here to create stacks of supplies visible on top of the bank to the left, probably for the Supply Depot.

Mesopotamia. Two Holt caterpillars, with extra canvas providing shelter from the sun. The black cat sign just visible between the two groups of men indicates that the tractors belong to 789 Company, which supported 157 Heavy Battery Royal Garrison Artillery, based on Samarah.

Mesopotamia. To be honest, the driver is showing off with this 'wheelie', fun but unwise.

Mesopotamia. A Holt caterpillar and 60-pounder gun with limber are being loaded onto a barge, probably to cross the River Tigris.

Salonika. A Model 'T' Ford and an ambulance in Salonika in 1917. ASC lorries can be seen in the background.

Salonika. Believed to be a scene on the coast of Salonika. Four Holt caterpillars are parked in a Nissen hutted camp; each caterpillar has a name painted on the top of the radiator: (left to right) 'The Old Jumper', 'Wait and See', 'The Steam Plough' and 'Caspian Star'.

Salonika. Part of the ASC Depot in Salonika, showing GS wagons, accommodation tents and MT bays.

Salonika. Another part of the ASC Depot, with lines of reserve vehicles, with huts and tents in the background.

Salonika. A game of football between an ASC team and local civilians, watched enthusiastically by large crowds.

North Russia. A number of RASC Warrant Officers and NCOs of the North Russia Expeditionary Force in October 1919. The Warrant Officer sitting centrally has five Overseas Service stripes.

North Russia. Four mules, ridden by two ASC postilions, and an ambulance 'somewhere in Russia.'

Palestine. This photograph of 1006 Company in Jerusalem in 1918 represents in some ways a little known and therefore almost forgotten campaign against the Turkish Army. The ASC operated 1601 lorries, 1467 cars and vans, 530 ambulances, 288 caterpillar tractors, with 1094 officers and 17817 Other Ranks in this campaign. There are five officers and fifty-four Other Ranks in the group, along with four dogs that look part of the same family.

Waziristan. 'The First Convoy into Razani Camp' (see footnote 63).

Footnotes

1: 'The Tramlines'. The two low parallel buildings visible in this photograph were called 'The Tramlines'; at that time they housed the HQ of the Service Companies and had various occupants over the following years (including the author of this book as Adjutant of 11 Training Regiment Royal Corps of Transport when the old redbrick barracks were pulled down in the late 1960s, to be replaced by unfriendly concrete and glass buildings). Buller Barracks, after being the home location of the Corps since the late 1850s, is about to be torn down and replaced by a civilian housing estate.

2: Gale & Polden. The firm was originally started by James Gale in 1866 in Chatham, Kent, joined in 1875 by Thomas Polden. In 1888, the firm moved to Wellington Street in Aldershot, close to the railway station, producing newspapers, books, postcards and a wide variety of stationery items, including Queen Mary's Christmas card in 1916 and Aldershot Military Tattoo programmes from the 1930s onwards. Above all, the firm was known throughout the Army for producing books on a wide range of military subjects, especially books to help individuals and units on educational and administrative matters. If you wanted to get on in the Army, Gale & Polden had the books to help you. In 1981, unfortunately, Robert Maxwell gained control of Gale & Polden and closed it down in November of that year.

3: Motor Volunteer Corps (MVC). The idea of a Corps of Motor Volunteers emanated in 1900 from members of the Army MT Committee, who suggested it was sponsored by the Automobile Club of Great Britain (later the Royal Automobile Club (RAC), see footnote 26). To demonstrate that such Volunteers could be beneficial for the Army, Mr Mark Mayhew, a founder member and Vice-President of the Automobile Club of Great Britain and who had served briefly in 1899 as a Lieutenant in the Middlesex Imperial Yeomanry, arranged for prominent members to put their cars at the disposal of Field Marshal Lord Roberts and his staff during an inspection of military stations in Kent in 1902, support that was highly praised by Lord Roberts. After further support was provided, the **Motor Volunteer Corps (MVC)** was formed in May 1903, with Mr Mark Mayhew appointed as Commanding Officer in the rank of Lieutenant Colonel, his headquarters being in Sackville Street, London. Successful enrolment enabled five Commands to be established, in London, Aldershot, Salisbury, York and Scotland. Pay was to be thirty shillings a day with an annual grant of £2.00 and ten days call out a year authorised. The Army autumn manoeuvres of 1903 were the first major commitment, followed in 1904 by the manoeuvres near Clacton-on-Sea. By this time, motor cycles had been added to the Corps, making its establishment 203 officers and men, including 40 motor cyclists, however, recruitment had not been totally successful, ostensibly because owner-drivers did not like being described as Privates.

To solve this difficulty, the MVC was disbanded in July 1906 and reformed immediately as the **Army Motor Reserve (AMR)**, with all its officers being initially accepted, although the AMR asked immediately for a reduction in their permanent staff, which caused problems. The AMR continued the good work of the MVC for some years but, as the Army acquired more cars and motor cycles and the clouds of war gathered, the need for the AMR was progressively reduced, much to their dismay. Eventually, the Army Council decided that the AMR should be disbanded, which was approved by the King on 31 October 1913, with disbandment on 1 November 1913.

4: Brodrick Caps. A new style of forage cap was introduced by the Army in 1902, named after the then Secretary of State for War, St John Brodrick. It was in the form of a dark blue, stiffened, round shaped forage cap, with no peak. It proved to be unpopular with the troops and was replaced by a broad-topped cap with a wired brim and leather peak in 1905, but it continued to be worn until 1908 within the ASC.

5: Laffan's Plain. Laffan's Plain was the flat Army training area between Aldershot and Farnborough on which major parades for Royalty and other distinguished men took place in Victorian times and until the First World War, named after Major General Sir Robert Laffan, late Royal Engineers (1821–1882). He was one of the officers responsible for the plans of the Infantry barracks in Aldershot and many improvements in the camp, including the planting of trees and the laying of turf during the very early days of construction of the barracks in the late 1860s when he was Commander Royal Engineers Aldershot. In 1887, he was later appointed Governor and Commander-in-Chief of Bermuda. Laffan's Plain was used increasingly for flying after 1918 and Army training was eventually stopped. It is now a commercial airport.

6: Tommy Atkins. Tommy Atkins, or sometimes just Tommy, has been used for many years, particularly by foreigners, denoting a soldier of junior rank in the British Army. While today we associate the name really with the First and Second World Wars, its origins go back much further: there is reference to its use in Jamaica in 1743, to 1794 when the Duke of Wellington referred to the bravery of a soldier in Flanders, to 1815 when the name was used as specimen names in documents, or even during the so-called Mutiny in India, mentioned in the book 'Sepoy Rebellion' by the Reverend EJ Hardy and in an 1892 poem by Rudyard Kipling. There are other references too, so it would be an unwise man who claimed a definitive source of this name.

7: Aldershot Ovens. These are simple ovens, which have been used for well over 100 years, ideal for field conditions. They are constructed from a semi-circle of corrugated iron, covered on three sides by turfs dug locally, the fourth side being the entrance, closed during cooking. They measure some five feet by three feet and need two to four hours to heat up; using 150lbs of wood a day, they will cook fifty-four loaves or dinners for 220 men at any one time.

8: God's Acre. The Recreation Ground in Buller Barracks, Aldershot was used as the sports ground for the barracks from the late 1850s. It suffered from being on a slight slope, which was then levelled and enlarged in 1893 under the direction of Colonel Grattan, Staff

Sergeant Major Rose and men of 18 Company ASC (HT). In due course, it hosted many Corps sports activities, including the annual Corps Weekend, indeed became the recognised Corps home ground for cricket, hockey, football and rugby. After the Second World War, the ground became known as 'God's Acre', the reasons for which remain obscure today; certainly the privilege of walking across the field's immaculate surface was granted to few senior or important individuals. The name, however, was once challenged in the letters section of the RASC Journal but it was too ingrained in Corps custom and usage to be changed.

9: The ASC HQ Officers' Mess. The Officers' Mess in Buller Barracks, Aldershot has always been defined within the Corps as the ASC HQ Officers' Mess, the only one of all the Corps messes to be so described. This meant that any Corps officer, serving or retired, had the privilege of entering and using the mess without obtaining prior permission, which was not the case with other messes.

The mess set the standards for all other Corps messes. It contained the bulk of the Corps' silver and paintings. All officers, wherever they served in the world, paid a small monthly contribution to the HQ mess. The reason for this unique situation was that, since late Victorian times, Aldershot was always considered the most important ASC location, where the head of the Corps was located, important Corps functions took place there and major visitors were hosted.

10: Pushball. The game was invented in Massachusetts, USA in 1891 and was introduced in England in 1902, at the same time as pushball on horseback was also introduced, played only in military tournaments such as at Olympia. The game died out after 1918.

11: 'W' Square. When the red-brick barracks in South Camp (i.e. the area south of the Basingstoke Canal) were constructed in the early 1890s, they were laid out in lines, 'A' to 'Z', based on the outline of the wooden barracks developed from the 1850s. The Corps occupied 'X', 'Y' and 'Z' lines. The new red-brick barrack blocks, which lasted until the late 1960s, were erected on the drill squares of the old wooden-hutted barracks. By chance, the square in 'W' lines was not built on and 'W' Square was retained for parades by the ASC, which soon developed into the infamous drill square in Buller Barracks, Aldershot, a square that instilled fear in many an ASC (and RASC) soldier over the years, although its reputation was worse than its bite. The square was located next to the offices of the Service Companies and the Corps Band, with wagon and horse lines at the lower end.

12: Mounting/Dismounting Competition. After the end of the Boer War of 1899–1902, the ASC developed an entertainment for the Corps Weekend in Buller Barracks that involved competitions between GS wagon teams from different companies to see how quickly a GS wagon could be stripped (dismounted) and reassembled (mounted). An inspection of team members at different stages was part of the competition. This activity was immediately added to the programme of the Royal Naval & Military Tournament held at Olympia in London between 1903 and 1913. In reality it was only practical for Horse Transport Companies stationed in Aldershot and Woolwich to compete and, since Woolwich was the nominated training location for mounted skills and units, Woolwich units tended to win most years.

13: St George's Church. The Church of St George, located on Queen's Avenue close to Buller Barracks, was designed in 1892 by two military Engineers; Queen Victoria laid the foundation stone in June 1892, since when the church has been the Corps church for the ASC, RASC and Royal Corps of Transport, hosting the annual Service of Remembrance and many other Corps church occasions. It contains old Corps memorials and a Corps side chapel, as well as a number of attractive stained glass windows, of particular interest being the East window presented by the ASC in memory of officers and men who died in the 1899–1902 war in South Africa.

14: Army MT Committee. This War Office committee was formed in 1900, with represention from the major Corps involved, the Royal Artillery, Royal Engineers and Army Service Corps, to recommend to the War Office vehicles suitable for Army use. For example, when it became clear that motor cycles were needed in the Army, the Army staged motor cycle trials at Brooklands in Surrey after the 1911 Olympia Show, when ten machines were bought by the War Office MT Committee for the ASC to trial. The work and recommendations of the committee were decisive for the development of MT in the Army. The MT Committee in 1912, for example, consisted of Colonel HCL Holden (late RA) (President), Lieutenant Colonel A Slade Baker AOD, Major WE Donahue ASC, Major HG Stevenson DSO (War Office), Major HCF Cumberlege ASC, Captain HN Foster ASC and Captain AE Davidson RE (Secretary).

15: Colonel Sam Cody. Born in Iowa, USA in 1867, was a Wild West showman and an early pioneer of manned flight (his real name was Samuel Cody Cowdery and he should not be confused with Buffalo Bill Cody). His interest in flying started with designing manned kites, which were offered to the Royal Navy (who turned them down) and the Army (who briefly took them on); he became the Chief Instructor of Kiting at the Army Balloon Factory on Laffan's Plain in Farnborough; importantly, his flight on 16 October 1908 was recognised as the first official flight in the UK, even though his plane crashed. With varying success, Colonel Cody continued his trials with aircraft, balloons and kites, but he was killed on 7 August 1913 when his floatplane broke in half at 500 feet over Ball Hill in Farnborough. His coffin was carried on a gun carriage pulled by a team of ASC men and horses in a funeral procession seen by an estimated crowd of 50,000 to 100,000 who lined the route from his home in Ash Vale to the Aldershot Military Cemetery. He was buried with full military honours. His descendants still live in Aldershot.

16: The Baby Caterpillar. When the Baby Caterpillar was delivered from Grantham, Lincolnshire it took ten days to reach Aldershot from Grantham, during which time its corkscrew motion caused it to be nicknamed 'Rock & Roll'. It frightened many a horse *en route*, so a funnel was added to make the horses think it was the sort of steam tractor they were used to seeing (some hope!). While the Baby Caterpillar answered many of the mobility problems faced by the Corps, the War Office decided in 1911 that there was no future for tracked vehicles in the Army, a decision that was rapidly reversed early in the First World War. The caterpillar in this photograph took part in the 1933 Royal Tournament, driven by the son of one of the original drivers and was retained by the Corps until the 1950s.

17: The Fowler Accident. This accident took place on a bridge over the River Arrow in Herefordshire, when the engine was towing two wagons of gas cylinders for an Army ballooning exercise. The outing to Herefordshire was the final part of a Royal Engineers course in Aldershot, with Colonel Cody one of the instructors.

18: Lower Establishment. This means that the Company is at cadre strength in officers, men and vehicles, well below what it would be on wartime establishment. In some ways it was an economic measure, but it did at least retain a serving unit when sufficient manpower was not available or necessary for a fully established unit.

19. The Territorial Force Reorganisation. Until 1908, there had been a few independent Army Service Corps Horse Transport Companies, notably the Hampshire Brigade ASC Company, which was raised in Stockbridge in 1885, but in 1908 regimental organisations were introduced to support the Territorial Divisions throughout the UK, which resulted in fourteen Transport & Supply Columns commanded by Lieutenant Colonels and fourteen Mounted Brigades, with ASC Companies commanded by Majors.

20: Casey's Court. The name generally refers to a gang of unruly children and harks back to music hall days of the early twentieth century. 'Casey's Court' was the title of a twice-nightly 'crazy' comedy show launched by a famous actor named Will Murray, with a caste mainly of children who were beyond control. Two of the most famous 'children' were Charles Chaplin and Arthur Stanley Jefferson (later known as Stan Laurel).

21: Royal Naval & Military Tournament. The Grand Military Tournament and Assault at Arms tournament, a military tattoo and pageant, first took place in 1880 in the Royal Agricultural Halls in London, in the early 1900s in Olympia and finally in the Earls Court Exhibition Centre. It involved officers and men of the Regular and Auxiliary units of the British armed services in a series of displays and competitions. The ASC participated after the Boer War, initially with a display involving stripping GS wagons and re-assembling them against the clock. The routine of the mounting/dismounting competition was dictated by four whistle calls. Points were deducted or gained against the clock or by detailed inspection by officers of the ASC.

First Whistle: horses were unhooked and tethered, and the teams took off jackets and helmets and formed up behind the wagons. Twenty marks.

Second Whistle: wagons were stripped and piled neatly, with associated tools and equipment packed into sacks. Standard time: One minute. Sixty marks.

Third Whistle: Assemble wagons, hook up horses, fall in. Standard time: Two minutes, with time penalties.

Fourth Whistle: Teams fall out and dress. No marks allocated; points, however, were deducted for a variety of 'errors'.

22: The Guards' Dash to Hastings 1909. At a time when motor transport was in its infancy, the War Office was reluctant to change from horses as a means of transport, partly for cost reasons. There were few MT enthusiasts in the Army so the Automobile Association (AA) organised, in coordination with the War Office, the move of a 600-strong mixed battalion of the Brigade of Guards (Grenadiers, Coldstream and Scots Guards) from London to Hastings to prove that it was possible to move large numbers of troops by road, along with their ammunition, weapons and other equipment. The previous year, ninety-four omnibuses had moved troops from Hounslow to Shoeburyness, but that seemed to have minimal effect in the corridors of power. On this occasion, AA members were recruited with their cars to provide key support.

On a bitterly cold day on 17 March 1909, some 100 open cars carried the battalion south (taxis being hired by the War Office for the ammunition etc), with crowds lining the streets to cheer them on. Arrival in Hastings was the highlight of the day, with the town populace out in full and bunting and flags hung from many buildings. Importantly, drivers and Guardsmen were provided with a hot meal through the generosity of the citizens of Hastings; and the exercise was adjudged to have been a great success.

23: Airline Units. These strangely-named units were employed to deploy Royal Engineer communication links raised above ground in manoevres or in wartime so that passing vehicles did not damage or destroy them. The worst offenders in damaging communication links laid across roads were tracked vehicles, of which the ASC had a good number, wheeled lorries and GS wagons too.

24: Territorial Force Efficiency Stars. The Corporal standing on the left of this photograph is wearing four Territorial Force Efficiency Stars on his right sleeve. He looks like an old soldier, certainly compared with the young Territorials on the right.

The basic Efficiency badge since 1881 appears to have been a lozenge-shaped cloth badge, which was awarded to Volunteers who were deemed as 'efficient in rifle drill and practice' in the last annual return of their Corps. After five (later four) years of being reported on as 'efficient', a star was awarded, which was worn above the lozenge. If, between then and the award of a second star, the Volunteer was not adjudged to be 'efficient' he was not allowed to wear the lozenge but could retain the star. After five (later four) years, a second star replaced the lozenge; subsequently every five (later four) years, another star was added. The Corporal in the photograph appears to have earned stars as an 'efficient' soldier for between sixteen and twenty years, depending on when his stars were awarded.

The initial TF Regulations in 1908 authorised the wearing of the lozenge and stars, but they appear to have been discontinued in 1914 as the TF Regulations in that year did not mention them.

The colour of the lozenge was appropriate to the facings of the Corps.

25: YMCA. The Young Men's Christian Association is a world-wide organisation, formed in 1844 in London, although it developed strongly thereafter in America. Its aim was to put Christian principles into practice by developing a healthy 'body, mind and spirit'. During the First World War, the YMCA established huts in every camp in the UK and in due course on the Western Front as well as in other theatres of war, providing home-type facilities for the troops, at the same time acting as the focal point for camp activities and religious services. 250 canteens were founded in UK within ten days of the declaration of war and the first YMCA contingent went to France in November 1914; some 1,500 YMCA workers were in France and Belgium at any one time, working in over 300 centres. After the Armistice in 1918, the YMCA provided free meals for 70,000 prisoners-of-war and continued to support the Army during the Occupation of the Rhineland.

26: National Motor Volunteers (NMV). After the disbandment of the Army Motor Reserve on 1 November 1913, there were no official Volunteer organisations to provide support to the Army, yet there was no shortage of people keen to 'do their bit' during the war, even if they were medically unfit or otherwise ineligible for the Forces.

The Royal Automobile Club and the Automobile Association were the two main permanent civilian organisations with an involvement in vehicles, mainly cars, and they, through their members, did magnificent work in providing cars for the Army. The problem was that the Army needed more than just cars; they needed lorries as well. A large variety of units and organisations appeared soon after the start of the war and the War Office experienced great difficulty in controlling them all but, early in 1915, Sir Charles Higham and Mr F Norman Wright were persuaded that it would be useful to organise bodies of like-minded motorists across the country into one organisation as part of the Volunteer Training Corps, recognised by the War Office as the National Motor Volunteers, to be employed within the UK in duties connected with home defence. It was a significant success, which probably indicates that the disbandment of the Army Motor Reserve at the end of 1923 was somewhat premature, if not inadvisable.

A major development in 1917 was that an NMV squadron, consisting of a Light Section and a Heavy Section, should be the basic unit at county level, their primary duty being the provision of transport to Volunteer Infantry Battalions. In the event, it was found that Light Sections were not needed in all of the squadrons. One of the first County Motor Volunteer Corps squadrons to be formed was the East Yorkshire Motor Volunteers, based in Hull with both a Light and a Heavy Section. Uniforms were not issued, but many men bought their own; some members wore (unofficially) the ASC cap badge. These County Motor Volunteer Corps units survived until the end of the war, when they became part of the ASC MT (V) (Motor Transport Volunteers) but they had all been disbanded by 1920.

27: Imperial Service Badge. The Territorial Force Imperial Service Badge was awarded to members of the Territorial Force who volunteered to serve abroad for the defence of the British Empire. It was introduced in 1908 on the creation of the Territorial Force, which was intended for service in the UK only, so that no Volunteer in the TF could then be forced to serve abroad. The badge was worn above the right breast pocket. It is mainly in postcards that these badges can be seen, either just before the First World War or during the first year of it. The badge was officially discontinued in 1921 when the Territorial Force was retitled the Territorial Army.

28: York Military Sunday. This parade commemorates the death of General Gordon of Khartoum on 26 January 1885, killed by the Dervish forces of the Mahdi. The parade, which involved bodies of soldiers and military bands, was discontinued at the start of the Second World War.

29: Army Football Challenge Trophy 1914. The Army's premier trophy was first instituted in 1888, with its permanent home the new Army Football Ground in Aldershot; the first winners were the 2nd Battalion the Argyll & Sutherland Highlanders.

The ASC, represented by the Woolwich football team, won it for the first time on Wednesday 13 April 1914, having *en route* been victorious against the 2nd Battalion The Scots Guards (5–3), 3rd Battalion The Coldstream Guards (5–1), the 19th Hussars (2–0), 2nd Battalion The Royal Sussex Regiment (2–0), 2nd Battalion The Royal Irish Rifles (4–0), and the 2nd Batttalion The Sherwood Foresters (2–0). In the final they beat the 1st Battalion The Hampshire Regiment (the favourites) 1–0. The goal was scored in the thirty-eighth minute by Sergeant Williams, who dribbled the ball down the right wing before cutting in and shooting from almost 40 yards into the top left of the goal, over the goalkeeper's head.

The match was attended by King George V, Queen Mary and other members of the royal family, also some 20,000 spectators. The Queen presented the Warwick Vase to Lieutenant Colonel CS Dodson, Commanding Officer ASC Woolwich, along with a smaller silver replica for permanent retention (still retained by The Royal Logistic Corps, successors to the ASC, RASC and RCT).

Members of the team were: (forwards) Sergeant Williams, Lance Corporal Houghton, Corporal Grist and Private Butler; (half backs) Sergeant Gibb, Private Hushar and Corporal Rowe; (full backs) Sergeant Cooper (Team Captain), and Lance Corporal Newbury; (goalkeeper) Lance Corporal Bird; (reserve) Lance Corporal Launchbury; and (trainer) RSM Hoppin.

After the presentations, the team was hosted by the Officers' Mess, Sergeants' Mess, Corporals' Mess and Men's Canteen in Buller Barracks, Aldershot before they made their weary way back to Woolwich by train, where they were met by the Mayor of Woolwich and others who entertained them in the nearby Royal Oak Hotel before they were allowed to return to their barracks in Grand Depot Road. Next day was back to work.

30: Grove Park. Grove Park was built in 1899–1902 as a workhouse, but the buildings became empty in 1904 and were requisitioned by the ASC in September 1914 for use as a selection and training depot for MT trades, also for the repair and issue of vehicles and the dispatch of units overseas. It became a major establishment for the training and testing of the ASC in mechanical trades, soon to be complemented by the addition of various outstations and the establishment of Osterley Park as a centre for MT training.

31: The London General Omnibus Company (LGOC). The LGOC diverted a number of their experienced drivers to train a large number of drivers at the start of the war, which helped with the pressure on the ASC to man an ever-expanding fleet of vehicles. The drivers were accommodated either in tents at Osterley Paark or in various lodgings in the Hounslow area; they marched to their vehicles which were parked on local public roads. The photograph shows eight trainees, the standard number for one instructor for a day's training, and an LGOC instuctor. The postcard printers occasionally wrote imaginative captions on the cards.

32: Pears Fountain, Isleworth, west London. This photograph shows the leading vehicles in a line of ASC lorries, with trainees waiting to start their day's driver training with LGOC instructors at the junction of the London Road and Spring Grove Road. Between the omnibus and the front vehicle can be seen Pears Fountain, which was presented in 1899 by Andrew Pears, who owned Pears Soap Works on the London Road. The fountain was removed in 1937 to make way for the new Heston Fire Station, but its whereabouts today are not known.

33: Osterley Park. The original manor house in west London was built in the 1570s, but the present building is a transformation in the eighteenth century by Robert Adam. After the outbreak of war in 1914, an ASC training establishment had been opened in Grove Park in south-east London, but this proved inadequate for the huge numbers of men needed by the ASC, so the grounds of Osterley Park were taken over in September until after the war for recruits who were to undergo driver training. With no parking space available within the house grounds, recruits had to march to their vehicles parked on local roads as far away as Hounslow. Accommodation for the trainees consisted of row upon row of 16-man tents and some huts.

34: Good Conduct Stripes. Originally authorised in March 1881, they were large stripes worn point-up on the left sleeve by soldiers up to the rank of Corporal or equivalent. Qualifying times were:

1 stripe:	2 years
2 stripes:	6 years
3 stripes:	12 years
4 stripes:	18 years
5 stripes:	23 years
6 stripes:	28 years

The definition of Good Conduct was complicated, but was largely based on qualifying service free from entries in the Regimental Conduct Book. In 1901, a soldier was recorded when discharged as having nine stripes, admittedly after fifty years service.

35: Wound Stripes. Wound Stripes, in gold Russia braid, were first authorised in August 1916, back-dated to 4 August 1914, as a dress distinction granted to soldiers who had been wounded in combat and whose names appeared in official casualty lists, one stripe for each time a man was wounded. They were worn on the lower left sleeve of a Service Dress jacket, below Good Conduct Stripes if awarded. The Wound Stripe itself was vertical, two inches long, initially made of brass, but generally seen in cloth. They were also awarded for 'gas wounded' and 'shell shock wounded' men, but not for accidental or self-inflicted wounds. Wound Stripes were discontinued in November 1922.

36: Overseas Service Stripes. The Army introduced Overseas Service Stripes in December 1917, worn point-up on the lower right arm of the Service Dress jacket. The first (bottom) stripe was red in colour for those whose overseas service started before 31 December 1914, while any successive stripes were blue. Periods of leave of less than a month in the UK still counted, so long as the soldier returned overseas at the end of his leave. Prisoners-of-war were initially not eligible for the Overseas Service Stripes, but this was later changed. Overseas Service Stripes were made retrospective to 4 August 1914 and were discontinued on 9 May 1920, with wear authorised until 1922.

37: Kitchener's Knuts. The word 'Knuts' was used by the Volunteers in 1914–1915 for those men who were among the 500,000 raised at the request of Field Marshal Earl Kitchener of Khartoum, the highly regarded Secretary of State for War, to create six new Divisions, popularly called Kitchener's Army. Individuals liked to call themselves Kitchener's Knuts. Some men in 206 Company served in Park Royal in London for a time and it appears that they too liked the name Knuts. Note that the front men, probably others too, are wearing heavy leather leg protectors on their right legs, used by riders of horses drawing GS wagons. It is not clear why one man is holding a rifle.

38. Model 'T' Fords. Henry Ford is famous for insisting that buyers could have any colour of Model 'T', so long as it was black. He is also known as being reluctant to sell his cars to European countries during the war, but he eventually relented and agreed to their use as ambulances. In total, over 125,000 Model 'T's were built by Ford for use by the Army. The British operated a fleet of of almost 19,000 lightweight Model 'T's during the war, mainly in the Middle East, with especial success in Mesopotamia, where they were used as ambulances, light patrol cars and even converted for use on railways. The Model 'T' was built under licence in Manchester in 1916–1917.

39: The Star & Garter Hotel, Richmond. When the work load in Grove Park grew too big and before Osterley Park camp opened in late 1914, the Star & Garter Hotel in Richmond was taken over temporarily to provide ASC men with basic training, with outstations in a number of other locations, including Lord's Cricket Ground. This photograph shows Captain Townson and the No 2 Company group at the Star & Garter Hotel.

40: Blackheath Knuts. A group of men at the No 2 Reserve Horse Transport Depot in Blackheath called themselves 'Blackheath Knuts'. The depot's task was to 'turn out' Horse Transport units ready for service anywhere, complete with officers, NCOs and men, animals and GS wagons, a system which was quite different from the one used in the MT side of the Corps. Almost 1,100 officers and over 28,000 men were trained at Blackheath over the period April 1915 to October 1917. Infantry and Machine Gun Corps men from Grantham were also trained at Blackheath.
(Did you notice the face in the window?)

41: Major General FWB Landon. Frederick William Bainbridge Landon was born on 27 February 1860 in Ledsham, Yorkshire and commissioned in 1879 into the West Riding Regiment. He transferred to the ASC in 1889, eventually becoming Inspector of the ASC in 1909–1912 in the rank of Brigadier, before promotion to Major General in 1913 as the Director of Transport & Movements in the War Office, then subsequently Inspector of ASC and QMG Services in 1914, an appointment he retained during the war until his retirement in October 1919. He had the final say in deciding on a unit's standard of efficiency before it could deploy overseas. He died on 26 October 1937.

42: 244 Company Sign. The company claimed to be the first ASC Company to introduce unit signs, in their case three intertwined fish, said to be an adaptation of the arms of their home county of Surrey, seen here on the scuttle on the right. On the same scuttle is stencilled 'B117', the bus number used by the LGOC. The Company sign can better be seen in the next photograph.

43: 244 Company leaving Holcombe in February 1915. The convoy has stopped just south of Holcombe, on Nettlebridge Hill between Stratton and Oakhill, probably for this impressive photograph or to ensure that the convoy was complete. Such spacing would have been impossible on the move; in any event men can be seen standing around at the bottom centre of the photograph.

44: A Break in Honiton, Devon. A column of American-manufactured White lorries takes a break in the centre of Honiton, Devon, where the scene has hardly changed since 1915. Thirteen lorries and some seventy ASC soldiers possibly represent a section of men on posting. Two lorries near the front have their bonnets up so may be experiencing engine problems. The convoy will wait for repairs to be completed before they move on.

45: Subsidy Scheme. This was a German idea, which was introduced by the British Army in 1908, originally for steam traction engines only. The intention was to make up for the shortage of vehicles held by the Army before the war by inviting vehicle operators, from 1911 onwards, to sell their vehicles to the Army if and when war broke out, initially with a subsidy of £38.00 or £52.00, depending on the class of vehicle, although these amounts were raised in 1914 to £120.00, payable in four instalments over three years.

Manufactureres who took part in the scheme were Albion, Dennis, Hallford, Karrier, Leyland, Maudslay, Thornycroft and Wolseley. Inevitably, this variety of manufacturers produced a wide range of vehicles, which led to huge spares problems at a later stage. As time went by, however, the demands of the War Office MT Committee increased, but vehicle manufacturers became less interested in supplying the Army because of the increasingly profitable use by civilian firms of motorized transport.

A number of Glasgow-built Halley lorries were requisitioned during the war, but were never popular in the Army. They were not part of the subsidy scheme, which was intended to encourage standardization. This photograph shows ASC men and a Halley lorry of the 1st (Cavalry?) Division in England.

46: Women's Legion. In July 1915, Lady Londonderry launched the Women's Legion, which became the largest body of civilian volunteers involved with war work. Strangely enough (and probably advantageously), it was not under the control of the government or the Army, nevertheless its members were keen to involve themselves in many forms of work. In April 1916, a motor transport section was authorised and numbers quickly rose so that, by August that year, 2,000 women were employed as drivers with the ASC. Because of the difficulty and dangers in using starting handles on normal lorries, they were mainly employed on driving light cars and ambulances.

As an example, 606 Company ASC, attached to the Ministry of Munitions in London, largely consisted of Women's Legion drivers, who drove ambulances, cars, vans and motorcycles with side cars.

In this photograph are eighteen members of the Women's Legion (out of a total of 150) in 613 Company, which was formed in January 1916 in Chester, before moving to Liverpool as the 25th Local Auxiliary (MT) Company, covering Cheshire, Cumberland, Gloucestershire, Lancashire and Wales. They are wearing ASC cap badges and shoulder titles, with Women's Legion collar badges.

Only after the Armistice in November 1918 were Women's Legion drivers employed abroad, particularly in the Occupation of the Rhineland, to assist in the early demobilisation of male drivers.

47: Donated Ambulances. At the start of the First World War, the horse-drawn ambulance was the standard means of transporting casualties, even though motorized trials had been held before the war and a few ambulances were held by units in the UK (three each in Aldershot Command and Irish Command, two each in Southern Command and Eastern Command, and one each in Northern Command, Western Command and Scottish Command, a total of thirteen); one motorised ambulance was held also in Egypt and South Africa.

Unfortunately, the Retreat from Mons in 1914, which involved action and movement by day and night, led to horses being overwhelmed and underfed, which in turn highlighted the necessity of motorized ambulances being introduced as a matter of extreme urgency. A public appeal for an ambulance fund drew enormous support and within weeks donations had reached £9,000.00 and promises had been received for 143 ambulances. Soon charitable organisations, commercial companies, societies and universities were raising money for ambulances; public generosity within the UK was extraordinary, quickly followed by support from America and the British Empire.

Some interesting donors were: The Association of Saint Peter's Collegians of South Australia, The Boilermakers and Shipbuilders Society, British Esperantists, the Children of Nova Scotia, the City of Calcutta (fifty ambulances), Domestic Servants of England Fund, the Fair Maid of Perth, Hea Swee Lee, Hellenic Committees of London and Liverpool, Natal Farmers, North Caucasian Oilfields, Members of the Pytchley Hunt, the People of Jamaica (also of Barbados, Bahamas, Fiji, Hong Kong and Shanghai), Rag, Scrap, Metal and Waste Trades, the Spiritualists of Great Britain, Toungoo District in Burma, United Provinces of India, various Districts in New Zealand and the Worshipful Company of Fishmongers.

Donated ambulances carried the names of the donors on the side of the ambulances.

48: Organisation of a Divisional Train. An ASC Divisional Train had four Transport Companies: No 1 (HQ) Company and Number 2, 3 and 4 Transport Companies. The No 1 (HQ) Company provided support for Divisional HQ and some small Divisional units; the other three companies supported their Brigades, an allocation that was occasionally changed during the war for operational reasons. This numbering of the companies goes back to 1908 before which time the Brigade title was used (e.g. The Black Watch Company); on the outbreak of war in 1914, all companies were numbered within the ASC Order of Battle, so that, for instance, No 3 Company in the 20th Division was 196 Company ASC, but it is not unusual sometimes to find the pre–war description used during the war, in spite of the confusion this could cause.

49: Pierrots. The history of pierrots goes back at least to the seventeenth century, when they were key characters on stage, sad but very human. Pierrots appeared for the first time in England in 1717, in a pantomime and in different guises, but gradually developed into clowns in the 1800s, appearing predominantly in music hall and the circus, before fading out between the two World Wars. The appearance of pierrots (as clowns) in Army units in the First World War is perhaps not surprising, as the typical soldier's sense of humour took perfect advantage of the varied types of characters that were written into unit entertainments; the opportunity of making fun of more senior personalities in the unit without getting into trouble was of course too good to miss.

50: Cookery in the Army. The earliest Cookery School to train Army cooks was established in Buller Barracks, Aldershot in 1907. Messing was the responsibility of the ASC, who subsequently operated a number of Cookery Schools in the UK. The instructors in this photograph were ASC, but a number of Rifle Brigade and Fusilier cap badges can be seen among the students. Three different demonstration ovens can be seen in front of the group.

51: Women's Forage Corps. A War Office Forage Committee was formed in 1915 for the supply of forage and other farm produce for the troops at home and overseas; this was especially important for the Western Front as war conditions meant that local supplies of forage had soon been exhausted and hay had to be sent from the UK base.

Six Forage Companies were formed in England and one each in Scotland and Ireland. Company members (women) were attached to the ASC, becoming the Women's Forage Corps. The Corps eventually reached a strength of 6,000 in the UK (they did not work on the Western Front or elsewhere abroad). The work involved baling, forking hay into machines, wiring, tying and weighing bales of hay, forage for Army horses. The Corps was administered by General HG Morgan at its HQ in Whitehall Court, London, with Mrs Athole Stewart as Superintendant of Women.

There were five grades of workers: Industrial Members, working in gangs of six; Horse Transport Drivers who transported their loads on GS wagons to the nearest railway station; Forwarding Supervisors, who checked the weight of bales and supervised loading at railway stations; Section Clerks, who dealt with all forage correspondence; and Quartermistresses, who drove Mechanical Supervisors on their rounds of inspection of hay baling machines, and distributed rations.

The dress for the Women's Forage Corps was khaki and green, with 'FC' shoulder titles. The cap badge consisted of the letters "FC" within a wreath on a star, but ASC cap badges were often worn.

52: Foden Thresh Disinfectors. The Foden Thresh Disinfector steamer, with two engine-driven ovens, was designed to kill bugs in soldiers' clothing; unfortunately it did not kill the bugs' eggs. The bulldog sign to the right of the Corporal (in the next photograph) indicates that this vehicle is in a 6 Corps MT Company. Thresh was a company which took out a patent for an improved disinfector, which was built in Keighley, West Yorkshire. The Army used ninety-eight such steamers.

53: 978 Company in Claydon, Suffolk. This unit was formed in September 1917 as 74 Local Auxiliary (MT) Company, commanded by Major TR Nuttall. It was located in the two large corrugated sheds of an old iron foundry. On formation, the company had twenty-five officers, five Warrant Officers/Senior Ranks, fifty-two Corporals and 893 other ranks. The Company was responsible for providing support to all MT units north of the River Thames and south of the line from Haverhill near Cambridge to Aldeburgh in Suffolk. The company was responsible for 1,100 vehicles in its area.

54: 56 Company Officers Take Tea. Officers of 56 Company, 4th Divisional Train, take tea during the retreat from Mons. This photograph appeared on the front page of *Le Miroir* in Paris on 6 September 1914. Left to right: M. Levy (Interpreter), Captain LC Bearne (later Lieutenant Colonel, Albert Medal), Lieutenant LEA Dunphy, Lieutenant HP Raymond (later Colonel) and Second Lieutenant H Potts. Interestingly the French Interpreter wears an ASC cap badge; his glasses are filled in for security reasons.

55: The Indian Supply & Transport Corps. The spare wheel behind the second rider was quickly discontinued in 1914, probably because of the lack of replacements. The Indian Army had arrived speedily in France but unfortunately they found the weather conditions extremely difficult and were transferred to the Middle East in 1916, after suffering 90,000 casualties.

56: A Leyland in France. A requisitioned Model BT Leyland in France early in the 1914 campaign, still showing it had been operated by the London & North Western Railway Express Parcels Service before the war. If it had survived long enough, the advert would have been over-painted khaki; without doubt the brakes need to be repaired or replaced (see the plank of wood wedged in by the front offside wheel to stop the vehicle moving).

57: Princess Mary's Christmas Box. Princess Mary's original intention, using her personal allowance, was to create a 'Sailors' and Soldiers' Christmas Fund' in order to ensure that every sailor afloat and every soldier at the front should receive a gift from 'home' on Christmas Day. This developed into a national appeal, which raised £162,591.00★ by the end of the war, predominantly in small donations from the ordinary people of Great Britain.

The box measured five inches long by three-and-a-quarter inches wide by one-and-a-quarter inches deep. The lid depicted Princess Mary's head in profile within a circle of laurel leaves, with her monogram 'M' on either side. Round the edge are the names of the allied countries, Belgium, Japan, Russia, Monte Negro and Servia in small roundels, with three furled flags represented on the left and right, a sword and scabbard along the top and the prow of two battleships along the bottom. In the centre of the bottom line are the words 'Christmas 1914'.

Each box contained a small picture of Princess Mary and a Christmas card, as well as a variety of useful items for soldiers in the field: a packet of twenty cigarettes or an ounce of pipe tobacco; non-smokers received a packet of acid drops; some boxes contained a writing case and pencil. Gurkhas received the same as British soldiers, Sikhs received sugar candy and a box of spices, Bhistis (from northern India) received a larger box of spices and other Indian troops received cigarettes, candy and spices. Nurses were treated to a packet of chocolate and the Christmas card, since smoking was not then considered a socially acceptable habit in which well brought-up women indulged.

The response to Princess Mary's Christmas Fund was so overwhelming that eligibility was extended from the original date, Christmas Day 1914, to include all British and Imperial military personnel who arrived later on the Western Front and in other theatres of war. When supplies ran out (ultimately 2.6 million★ boxes were distributed compared with the initial assessment for the first seven Divisions of the British Expeditionary Force), a selection of the following was sent: brushes, bullet pencil cases, combs, knives, pencil cases, purses, scissors and tobacco pouches. Recipients included the wounded, whether in hospital or on sick leave, and the widows or parents of those who had been killed; prisoners–of–war as well as internees received theirs when they were repatriated.

Although some 355,000★ boxes were delivered by Christmas Day, the difficulties of production and distribution around the world unfortunately delayed delivery, often until at least 1916, some even after the Armistice in 1918. In fact, the War Office reported in January 1919 that some 252,000 boxes had still not been delivered and advertised in newspapers in the hope of contacting the remaining eligible soldiers.

The shortage of brass, needed for weapons and ammunition, also contributed to the delays. A large amount of brass was ordered from America, but 45 tons of it were lost in May 1915 when the Royal Mail Steamship *Lusitania* was sunk near Ireland during its voyage back from America. This shortage led to those boxes which were produced later in the war being of poor, thinner quality.

The fund was closed in 1920. The remaining money was transferred to the Queen Mary's Maternity Home, which supported the wives and children of servicemen.

★ Different sources give different figures.

58: The Auxiliary Omnibus Park. In 1917, a reorganization of ASC transport was initiated, to centralize all transport under Corps or General Headquarters control. An Auxiliary Omnibus Park was formed, containing all omnibus companies. At the same time, the companies were withdrawn to the coast for reorganization, refurbishment and some re-equipment, essentially providing twenty-five charabancs for each company. By early 1918, the Park was positioned in an arc behind the Corps and Divisions, ready for any tactical situation. When the Germans attacked on 21 March, the Park really showed its worth. Eighteen Divisions were moved to support the Army in opposing the German Army, with great success, carrying 211,213 men and travelling 855,638 miles in the process. Field Marshal Sir Douglas Haig authorised the immediate award of twenty-one Military Medals to members of the Park. A line of charabancs from an earlier move is illustrated here.

59: Red Cross Drivers. The left-hand man in this photograph is a Red Cross driver, while the other two are ASC. This may have been the moment when the ambulance was handed over to the ASC in late 1915 when Red Cross drivers had to chose between enlisting in the ASC and returning to England (fifty-six per cent transferred to the ASC).

60: Water Tanks in France. One of the tasks of the ASC was to assist the Royal Engineers in checking the quality of water to be consumed by the troops on the Western Front. The ASC provided the vehicles and the Royal Engineers the specialist skills. The unit sign of a spanner crossed with a glass retort can be seen above the cab. The driver appears to have collected a canine friend along the way.

61: The Red Coffee Bar. As coffee was almost an unknown drink in the United Kingdom at this time, a coffee bar represented a minor revolution. Why the description 'red' was used is not clear.

Many organisations provided canteens for the troops, but the Expeditionary Forces Canteens, with the ASC playing a large role, were the main providers from 1915 on, not only on the Western Front but also in the other theatres of war. 577 canteens opened on the Western Front in the war, providing station buffets, butcheries, cinemas, laundries, mineral water factories, officers' clubs, rest houses and sausage factories. Sixty-six canteens were destroyed during the March–April 1918 German assault.

62: The Rheinhotel Dreesen, Bad Godesburg, Bonn. Little did these Royal Engineers know that where they stood at the end of the First World War would have a strong link with personalities in the Third Reich.

Adolf Hitler himself liked to stay in the hotel during the 1930s, indeed is recorded as having stayed there on seventy occasions. It is thought that Rudolf Hess recommended the hotel. It was here in June 1934 that Hitler made plans to purge the Sturmabteilung Brown Shirts and murder its leader Ernst Röhm. Hitler met Prime Minister Neville Chamberlain here in late September 1938 and proposed the annexation of the Sudetenland in the Czech Republic, which was officially agreed at the Munich meeting in September. The annexation of the Sudetenland was one of the important steps leading to the Second World War.

63: Waziristan in India. Control of the Indian frontiers was the cornerstone of defensive strategy for British India in Victorian times, and the biggest threats were attempts by Russia to expand her empire in the late 1800s. The vehicles here appear to be modified load-carrying Model 'T' Fords, though the reason for going to Razani in Waziristan is not known. Razani is now a part of Pakistan.

Footnote to the Colour Section

58: Silks. The first silks appeared in 1898, just before the Paris Exhibition in 1900, and became very popular during the 1914–1918 war. A cottage industry provided silks for (mainly) British soldiers to send home as souvenirs from the British Expeditionary Force on the Western Front. Wives and family members in France and Belgium embroidered strips of silk organdie with sentimental or patriotic designs, flowers, flags, butterflies and, importantly, regimental badges; the completed strips were then sent to Paris for final assembly and distribution. It is believed that some ten million silks were sent during the war and that the first regimental badges on silks were initiated for the ASC. Not only were silks embroidered by hand but they were also, for more complicated designs (e.g. politicians and military leaders), woven by machinery. As the demand grew, however, production moved to factories in Paris.

The cards were produced in three forms, landscape-shaped, portrait-shaped and both these shapes with a pocket to cater for a small card. The cards came inside light-brown, thin, transparent envelopes but, due their vulnerability, the Forces Post Office would not post them unless they were sent in a separate envelope. Sometimes, a few words were written on the back of cards.

The production of silks ceased after 1923, but started again for the early years of the Second World War, when the British had little opportunity to acquire them, although examples do appear; silks, however, were still produced in small numbers for members of the German Army.

Index